IBSEN

HENRIK IBSEN

Painting by Eilif Peterssen

IBSEN

An Approach

by

JANKO LAVRIN

METHUEN & CO. LTD. LONDON
36 Essex Street, Strand, W.C. 2

First Published in 1950

CATALOGUE NO. 5199/U

PRINTED IN GREAT BRITAIN

ACKNOWLEDGMENT

Several chapters in this book are based on my previous study, *Ibsen and his Creation*, long since out of print.

Practically all quotations have been taken from Ibsen's *Collected Works*, arranged by William Archer (Heinemann). For the majority of extracts from letters and speeches I am indebted to *Ibsen's Correspondence* (Hodder and Stoughton) and *Speeches and Letters of Ibsen* (Frank Palmer). The three passages from Kierkegaard are taken from *A Kierkegaard Anthology*, ed. by Robert Bretall (Oxford University Press). To the publishers, translators and editors of the above-mentioned works my thanks are due.

J. L.

CONTENTS

*The frontispiece portrait of Henrik Ibsen by
Eilif Petersen is reproduced from a photograph
supplied by the Royal Norwegian Embassy.*

I

INTRODUCTORY

I

THE interest in a writer of Ibsen's stamp and magnitude is bound to fluctuate. And since in the aftermath of the Second World War Ibsen seems to have come—at least in this country—into his own again, one is perhaps justified in summing up the principal features of his work from the angle of an age which has justified some of his worst forebodings and apprehensions. This can only be done, however, by following the development of Ibsen the dramatist parallel with that of Ibsen the man. For it would be difficult to find another author whose work is so closely interwoven with his own inner quest, with his personal crises and aspirations, as is the case with Ibsen. At the same time he can best be understood if seen against the background of his own period—a period which he experienced and expressed mainly through opposing it all the time. Yet the first thing that strikes one in this greatest dramatist of our age is the fact that his external life was neither great nor dramatic in a spectacular sense, even though he lived through some of the highly dramatic happenings and changes in modern history.

Born in 1828, he saw in the course of his long life (he died in 1906) a series of happenings, the consequences of which could not but affect the future of Europe and indeed of mankind. The revolutionary outbursts in 1848 were greeted by him with all the verve of a youth of twenty, anxious to fight for a renewal of life. After a period of unavoidable reaction, there followed in rapid succession the Crimean Campaign, the abolition of serfdom in Russia, the Civil War in America, the Prussian victory over the Danes, and, some two years later, the Austrian debacle at Sadowa. Of even greater importance were the Franco-German War and the subsequent Prussianization of Germany; the rise of a united Italy; the Russo-Turkish War; the Berlin Congress; the rivalries of imperialistic powers for colonies and world-markets; and finally the Russo-Japanese War, which was interrupted by the first Russian revolution—an ominous prelude to a century seemingly intent on running amok amidst the chaos of its own disintegration.

No less conspicuous was the mental and social political fermentation after 1848. Apart from the growing struggle between the forces of liberalism and those of reaction, there was the rise of the national idea which, in some cases, assumed truly pathological proportions. The triumphs, and the ravages, of science also added their quota. The advent of the Darwinian theory in particular undermined, or threatened to undermine, a number of old inherited beliefs, including those religious and moral values of mankind which until then had been regarded as unshakable. In an atmosphere of restlessness and uncertainty there emerged a devastating sense of relativity, against which all the lingering rear-guard actions of the old ideas and ideals proved of little avail. At the same time the gap between the 'haves' and 'have-nots', between the capitalist bourgeoisie and the working classes, far from being bridged, was assuming the size of an abyss wide enough to engulf, at a none too distant date, an entire historical era.

It was with these disturbing processes at work that Ibsen's creative years coincided. Sensitive as he was to the spirit of the age, he could not but reflect them in his plays. Hence the various phases of Ibsen's writings may contribute to our understanding of certain inner workings of the age in which he lived; or at least of the advanced consciousness of that age. And as to the literary side of his dramas, they reflect *all* the principal schools and currents of the last century: from romanticism to realism, and from naturalism to the symbolist experiments of the *fin de siècle*. His rise to fame is the more interesting because he had to make his way upward from extremely narrow and petty surroundings with no outside aid or encouragement, until his efforts were crowned at last by a triumph which has made his name one of the greatest in the literature of our time.

II

Although a native of Skien—a small Norwegian town of some 3,000 inhabitants—Ibsen can hardly be called a 'racially' pure Norwegian. One of his ancestors, the sea-captain Peter Ibsen, was a Dane who at the beginning of the eighteenth century settled in Bergen and married a woman of German extraction. More German admixture was added during the subsequent generation.

There was also some Scottish blood in the family—all of which may or may not have contributed to the broad cosmopolitan tendencies of Ibsen's mind. Certainly his childhood and youth were passed in circumstances which were neither broad nor cosmopolitan. He was born into an atmosphere of fairly prosperous parochial respectability, with its 'mighty' men whose prestige rested above all on money derived from commerce and shipping. Ibsen's own father was one of them—at least until (in 1836) he went bankrupt and had to exchange his former affluence for an obscure existence in a farmhouse outside the town. Ibsen was a boy of eight when this happened; but he must have been painfully aware of the sudden reversal of fortune, as well as of the change in the style of life. The socially ostracized bankrupt, who crops up in several of his plays (Monsen in *The League of Youth*; Krogstad in *A Doll's House*; Hialmar's father in *The Wild Duck*; old Borkman in *John Gabriel Borkman*), may have been an echo of that early experience of his.

The reduced material circumstances not only made a great difference in the prospects of the boy's education and of his future in general, but also thwarted him emotionally. He seems to have conceived a strange aversion to his father and to his family in general, whom he neither cared to correspond with nor to revisit (except once), after he had left—at the age of sixteen—for Grimstad in order to earn his living as a pharmacy apprentice. Both Hialmar Ekdal in *The Wild Duck* and Mrs. Borkman in *John Gabriel Borkman* dream of restoring to honour the family name which has been ruined by a bankrupt father in the first case and by a bankrupt husband in the second. Ibsen may have had something similar in mind during his years of drudgery at Grimstad. As if determined to work his passage back to the same or even greater prestige than that lost by his father, he developed early enough a prodigious will-power and determination: this in a small provincial hole, where life was even more tedious than in his native Skien. His poverty and social insignificance were bound to foster in him almost at once an aggressive and warlike attitude towards his entire *milieu*. The only relief he was able to find was in writing satirical poems about local worthies. Occasionally he went out sketching, but he had neither the means nor the leisure to develop his talent as a painter. It was probably during those days that he first learned the baleful influence of such existence on one's healthy *joie de vivre*, which, in an atmosphere of this kind, could not but degenerate into clandestine dissipations and the wild oats mentioned by Mrs. Alving in *Ghosts*, when talking of her husband's youth.

Ibsen himself must have been sowing wild oats in those days simply because there was no alternative provided for a healthier relaxation. As a result of a love-affair (or whatever one may call it) with a maidservant ten years his senior, he became—at the age of eighteen—father of an illegitimate son, Hans Jakob, born in 1846. Usually glossed over, this fact must have had an enormous influence on Ibsen's mind and character, indeed on his entire development. The immediate reaction he had to endure on the part of the gossipy philistines, once they had become aware of such a *faux pas* committed by a youngster, can be imagined. So can the consternation in Ibsen's pietistic family. Any gaining of social prestige in such a 'respectable' community was now out of the question. The young culprit was willy-nilly driven into the camp of the rebels and critics, and the only attitude still left to him was that of defiant self-assertion against a society which he resented. Observant as he was, he knew by then all that was hidden behind the mask of conventional morality and did not mind saying it. It may have been largely the feeling of repressed shame that made him unwilling to have, from now on, any further contacts with his family. The rupture with them was so complete that the only member to whom he wrote a couple of letters during the rest of his life was his younger sister Hedvig. Much later, on hearing of his father's death (in 1877), he sent a few lines to one of his half-uncles, in which he tried to justify his silence by the fact that for a number of years he was unable to 'offer assistance of any kind' to his parents—surely a lame excuse.

The aversion to his kith and kin, to the entire atmosphere in which he lived, expanded into aversion to his native land in general—a mood which soon came out in his desire to settle in some distant foreign country or other. This does not mean that Ibsen wasted any love or affection on his illegitimate offspring. Far from it. He was compelled by law to contribute (for fourteen years) a certain sum towards the upkeep of his child, and that was all. Otherwise he never took the slightest interest in him. But while shunning the responsibilities a decent father would have shouldered in such a case, he must have suffered from remorse, since his inner make-up was thoroughly Protestant and imbued with a Puritan sense of guilt almost as a matter of course. And where there is awareness of guilt and of eschewed responsibility, there must also be a feeling of impending retribution even when the deeper religious roots justifying such an attitude have been weakened or else destroyed. This brings us straight to some of Ibsen's basic themes in which the problem of moral guilt and retribution looms very large indeed. In no modern author does the 'guilt-complex', as well as the fear of retribution, play so big a part as in Ibsen's works. The number of illegitimate children, too, is surprisingly high in his dramas. So is the number of characters who suffer from a painful secret connected with some transgression in the past which they try to conceal, but in vain; it always comes out in the end. As every student of Ibsen knows, a typical Ibsenian play is really nothing but an 'epilogue', with the inevitable retribution following upon a fault committed in the past. Which means that even Ibsen's technical innovations in the drama may have been partly due to his own painful secret— the birth of his illegitimate son, Hans Jakob.

III

In spite of that, Ibsen's basic disposition was one of romantic and militant idealism. He ridiculed and castigated what he saw around not only from rancour, but also from a genuine desire to see a better world than the one he had to contend with. Both motives are conspicuous in his first play, *Catilina*—an immature declamatory work (with obvious traces of Schiller), inspired by the events of 1848 and written at Grimstad in the winter of 1848–9. Ibsen read the play to his friend, the law-student Schulerud, who was so enthusiastic over it that he took it to Christiania (now Oslo), firmly resolved to launch it there with success. As neither the theatre nor the publishers would have anything to do with it, Schulerud printed it at his own expense. The booklet appeared in the spring of 1850, when Ibsen, too, had seen the last of Grimstad and came to Christiania in order to prepare, in Heltberg's famous 'students factory', for matriculation. The two friends pinned their hopes on the financial returns of *Catilina*, but the booklet proved such a failure that neither the author nor the 'publisher' could afford to have lunch for weeks on end. At last they sold all the printed copies to a grocer, who used the paper to wrap his wares. As Ibsen remarks, this transaction enabled Schulerud and him to buy, for the time being, their much-needed daily bread.

Undaunted, the budding author continued his literary activity with that tenacity which he preserved to the end of his life. His second work, the romantic one-act play *The Warriors' Mound* (*Kjämpehöien*, 1850) was actually performed in the Christiania theatre, without, however, improving his financial position. Nor did his endeavours in the 'students factory' lead to anything, for he failed to pass the examination. On the other hand, Ibsen found among his fellow-students several youths, including Björnstjerne Björnson, who played a conspicuous part in his subsequent career. Björnson was five years younger than Ibsen. Others, Vinje, for instance, and Botten-Hansen, were not only older but more experienced and more mature. And since all of them happened to be in a similar state of mental ferment, young Ibsen derived from their company considerable benefit. He was also on the staff of the short-lived periodical *Andhrimner** (the name of the cook in Walhalla), edited by Osmund Vinje and Botten-Hansen. Among the satirical writings he contributed—in verse and in prose —to that paper, was the biting lampoon *Norma, or a Politician's Love*, based on the libretto of Bellini's opera. Still, his financial position remained as bad as ever.

Things began to look brighter for him when, in November 1851, he was offered the post of stage-manager and producer in the newly-established Norwegian theatre in Bergen. The six years he spent in that town were of vital importance for his development as well as for his subsequent career. It should be borne in mind that the principal theatre in Norway—in Christiania—was in those days Danish rather than Norwegian: with a Danish director, Danish actors, and even a predominantly Danish repertory. But that was to be expected. Having seceded, in 1814, from Denmark in order to become autonomous under the Swedish crown, Norway kept its traditional Danish-Norwegian literary language: the so-called *riksmaal* as distinct from the vernacular *landsmaal*. The Norwegian bourgeoisie, too, notably in the capital, adhered to Danish culture. The eighteenth-century Danish classic, Ludvig Holberg, known as the 'Scandinavian Molière', was really not a

---

* The periodical was modelled on the Danish *Corsaren*, which was so fiercely resented and attacked by Sören Kierkegaard.

Dane, but a Norwegian by birth. During the period of romanticism, however, whose leaders in Norway were the poets Welhaven and Wergeland, a gradual tendency towards a more independent Norwegian literature and culture became apparent. It may have been quite a legitimate reaction against cultural encroachment on the part of Denmark, and perhaps also against economic encroachment on the part of Sweden. In any case, (natural) con- *national ?* sciousness was in the ascendant, and one of its first important by-products was the *Norwegian* theatre, founded in Bergen by the famous violinist Ole Bull, who entrusted it to the guidance of the as yet utterly inexperienced Ibsen.

IV

Ibsen's official duty was to function not only as producer but also as *Dramaturg*, whose special task was to write, from time to time, a play in the fashion of the day. Adhering to that fashion, he concentrated on national-romantic or else folkloristic themes —partly under the influence of such well-established Danish playwrights as Oehlenschlaeger and Heiberg. History, folk-ballads, Icelandic sagas, Norwegian folk-tales—they all contributed to his early works, few of which achieved any marked success on the stage. His *St. John's Night* (*Sancthansnatten*, 1853) was a complete failure. Even his ambitious and skilfully constructed *Lady Inger of Östraat*, produced two years later, had a lukewarm reception. His lyrical and somewhat operatic *The Feast of Solhoug* (*Gildet paa Solhoug*, 1856), however, appealed to the audiences even if it failed to impress the critics. Some of these went so far as to charge the author with plagiarism—an accusation against which Ibsen defended himself as late as 1883 in the preface to the second edition of the play. After *Olaf Liljenkrans*, imbued, like *St. John's Night*, with folklore romanticism, but otherwise one of Ibsen's weakest plays (it was first printed only in 1898), Ibsen reached astonishing dramatic power in his laconic and ruggedly bracing *Vikings in Helgeland* (*Haermendene paa Helgeland*, 1858). He himself refers to it as the best paid of his early works; it brought him in the sum of £31.

All this, with the exception of his Shakespearian drama *The Pretenders* (*Kongsemnerne*, 1863), was only a prelude to the real or essential Ibsen, whose genius still had to find its proper material, as well as its proper channel. His heart was neither in

the folklore nor in that cult of an idealized romantic past which
can so easily become a pretext for running away from the present.
After all, Ibsen the dramatist wanted to come to grips with life.
So he took up—a year before *The Pretenders*—a contemporary
theme in his *Love's Comedy* (*Kaerlighedens Komedie*), undoubtedly
the most provocative of his early works.

Frustrated socially and economically, Ibsen had to struggle
hard for every advance he made. No wonder that in his case success
began to mean struggle as well as sacrifice. According to his ideas,
any step forward had to be paid for by some sacrifice or other,
and this attitude soon became the very basis of his philosophy of
life. In his poem, *On the Heights* (*Paa vidderne*), belonging to the
same period as *Love's Comedy*, Ibsen depicts a striving youth who
becomes a free dweller of the heights only after having voluntarily
sacrificed all the comforts of life, including his home and his
betrothed. The poem ends with these characteristic lines:

> Nu er jeg staalset, jeg fölger det bud,
> der byder i höiden at vandre!
> Mit lavlandsliv har jeg livet ud;
> her oppe paa vidden er frihed og Gud,
> derunde famler de andre.

> (Now am I tempered like steel; I follow that call
> which summons me to wander in the height!
> I have lived out my lowland existence;
> here on the moor there are freedom and God,
> down there grope the others.)

It was with the inner make-up of such a dweller on the heights
that Ibsen the dramatist eventually dared to attack and to criticize
the existence of those 'groping underneath'. In order to make
his voice the more effective, he first had to master all the secrets
of his art, and the years he spent in Bergen served him in good
stead. As he was entirely new to the *métier* when taking over his
duties, he was sent in the spring of 1852 on a study-journey to
Copenhagen and Dresden, famous on account of their theatres.
As a dramatist, Ibsen learned a great deal from the French plays,
notably those by Scribe and Sardou—with their compact plots,
their cleverly devised misunderstandings, and their art of dramatic
suspense. But he took advice from other quarters as well: from
H. T. Hettner's book, *Das moderne Drama* (1851), for instance,

some tenets of which he adopted to great advantage. He probably owed to it not only his propensity to make the *dramatis personae* typical of their age and generation, but also the frequent application of his own sense of *chiaroscuro*, through which the repressed painter in him asserted himself in terms of drama.

Judging by his drafts and diagrams, Ibsen must have taken his work as a producer very seriously. But whether he was really efficient in this capacity still remains a matter of doubt. For one thing, the underpaid black-haired and black-bearded little man was a bad mixer—much too inhibited, too shy and aloof to do full justice to his job. In this respect he was the opposite of his friend and rival, Björnson, who was at his best when surrounded (and admired) by other people. The actress Lucia Wolf, who had started her stage career under Ibsen, gave in her reminiscences a not too flattering portrait of her mentor. 'He was always kindly and polite,' she says, 'but in his kindness there was something which invariably made me, at any rate, finish my talk with him as quickly as I possibly could; one just asked the necessary question, one received the answer, and—that was all! I was simply afraid of him. Wrapped in his long cloak, he would pace all the time up and down and, if addressed by anyone, would retreat into that cloak like a snail into its shell. . . . He approved of our way of acting even when we acted rather badly, as we often did. Such lack of criticism we ascribed not to incompetence on his part, but rather to his tiredness or his amiability—especially with actresses, whom he always found excellent.'

Be this as it may, Ibsen benefited from his experiences at Bergen at least as dramatist. When in 1857 a Norwegian theatre was founded in Christiania (as a rival of the Danish stage in the Norwegian capital), Ibsen was offered its directorship, which he accepted. Once back in the capital, he married Susanna Thoresen—a step-daughter of the popular authoress Magdalene Thoresen. He proposed to her after two previous loves and wooings—also in Bergen—both of which had come to nothing. It is a well-known fact that when caught courting by the indignant father (the 'pillar of society' type) of one of the girls, Ibsen ran away like a coward, leaving her to face alone the wrath of her indignant parent. On the whole, Ibsen was much less courageous in life than in art, whereas his wife Susanna never shrank from practical difficulties. Her cheerful and patient character must have

been a godsend to him, especially during those years in Christiania
—the worst during the whole of his career. The theatre to
which he was now attached had been a shaky affair from the outset
and became even more so under Ibsen's management. Whatever
the reasons, there was a time when he seemed to have lost all
interest in his duties. This only hastened the failure of the whole
enterprise in 1862. Ibsen, whose family responsibilities had been
increased by the birth of a son (Sigurd), incurred so many debts
and financial worries that he had to be helped out by friends.
Among these the successful and self-confident Björnson was
always most generous. It was due above all to his endeavours
that, in spite of many obstacles, Ibsen at last obtained from the
government a meagre literary scholarship which enabled him to
leave Norway (in 1864) and to settle abroad—a change that was
full of incalculable consequences.

V

Quite apart from those deeper personal reasons and inhibitions
which urged him to shake the dust of his native land off his feet,
Ibsen was glad to escape from the petty, small-town atmosphere,
which he always hated and despised. Even the Christiania of
those days was a small town, or rather, an overgrown village. 'You
do not know to what a terrible degree I feel lonely up here,' he
wrote in August 1863 to the Danish critic Clemens Petersen. So
he was the more relieved to have exchanged it for the big world.
He first settled in Rome, where he stayed for just over five years.
Then he moved to Dresden. From 1875 on, he lived mostly in
Munich, while making prolonged visits to Italy, preferably to
Rome whose broad cosmopolitan tradition never ceased to
fascinate him.

The first-fruits of his Italian sojourn were *Brand* (1866) and
Peer Gynt (1867)—the two masterpieces which brought him
recognition in Scandinavia. He found Rome a particularly stimu-
lating place to work in and took full advantage of it. Even his
bulky philosophic-historical drama, *Emperor and Galilean*,
although completed much later (1873) in Dresden, had been
begun in Rome. It was there also that he probably conceived his
satirical comedy of manners, *The League of Youth* (*De unges
Forbund*, 1867), which caused the first big rift in the friendship
between Ibsen and Björnson.

Rancorous and morbidly touchy, like all people who are on the defensive, Ibsen suspected—unjustly—Björnson of having been partly responsible for an adverse criticism of *Peer Gynt*. Having misinterpreted the versatility of his literary rival in an unfavourable light he called him in a poem (*Nordens Signaler*) a 'weathercock on the tower'. He also endowed Stensgaard, the principal character of *The League of Youth*, with a few features reminiscent of Björnson. But these he distorted into demagogic propensities and unscrupulous social 'climbing'. Björnson himself, whether rightly or wrongly, saw in this comedy an attempt at 'assassination in the grove of Muses'. The quarrel which followed was not settled till 1892, when Ibsen's only son Sigurd married Björnson's daughter Bergliot.

After his Scandinavian success with *Brand*, Germany became interested in Ibsen's works, and he took good care that his own chances of success in that country should not be neglected or thrown away. Knowing the value of advertising, he wrote (in May 1869) to his first German translator, P. F. Siebold, as follows:

You are connected with the *Leipziger Illustrierte Zeitung*; if it were possible for you to get in a biography of me there, I could furnish the necessary portrait. Councillor Hegel* would furnish you with the necessary material. Such a biography ought to contain only favourable matter; the German critics will surely find enough that is objectionable later on. I should particularly like, in case you think it helpful, you to mention what I had to struggle against in the earlier days, and that you should also emphasize the fact that the Cabinet and Storthing, acknowledging the position I hold in Norwegian literature, several years ago unanimously granted me a pension for life, besides providing ample travelling stipends, etc.

All of which is exaggerated—to put it mildly. The grant had been neither ample nor unanimous, but autobiographical data need not be one hundred per cent true.

It is not unlikely that, after Rome, Ibsen settled in Germany with an eye on his growing success in that country, which was renowned for the high standard of its theatrical productions, especially those of the Meiningen group of actors who took up Ibsen's dramas from 1875 onwards. But strangely enough, each

---

* Frederik Hegel, the owner of the famous Gyldendalske publishing firm in Copenhagen where, owing to Björnson's intercession, Ibsen's works from *Brand* onwards appeared.

radical change of place seems to have affected his choice of themes, the atmosphere, and even the style of his plays. On leaving Norway, he said good-bye to his patriotic and national-romantic motifs. Italy was responsible above all for his two dramatized epics, *Brand* and *Peer Gynt*. In Dresden again he worked out not only his new technique, so momentous in the evolution of modern drama, but actually turned his plays into a perfect medium for those invectives and 'ideas' which he wanted to bring home to his audiences in Scandinavia, in Europe, and finally in the whole world. The series opened with *The Pillars of Society* (*Samfundets Stötter, 1877*), the topical touch of which seems to have been provided by Samuel Plimsoll's attacks, in the British Parliament, on the racket with unseaworthy ships or 'floating coffins' as they were called. The aggressive character of the two plays that followed, *A Doll's House* (*Et Dukkehjem,* 1879) and *Ghosts* (*Gengangere, 1881*), made Ibsen the most discussed and most abused author in Europe. As the attacks did not abate in virulence, he gave an answer in *An Enemy of the People* (*En Folkefiende, 1882*) with all the verve he was capable of. After *The Wild Duck* (*Vildanden, 1884*), however, his fighting temper subsided, giving way to his dissecting and analytical propensity.

Most of his plays from now on kept intriguing his contemporaries, and even more his critics, often to the great amusement of the author himself. The paradoxical themes, so full of ambiguities, of hidden or open symbolism, provided many a puzzle for his audiences. *Rosmersholm* (1886), *The Lady from the Sea* (*Fruen fra Havet,* 1888), *Hedda Gabler* (1890), *The Master Builder* (*Bygmester Solness,* 1892), *Little Eyolf* (1894), *John Gabriel Borkman* (1896), and *When We Dead Awaken* (*Naar vi döde vaagner,* 1899) are partly tragic monographs of individual conscience, and partly transposed confessions of the author himself. In some of the last plays, however, the element of confession prevails. So does that peculiar 'symbolist' flavour which Ibsen imparted to his work on his return to Norway in 1891.

VI

Ibsen had left Christiania at the age of thirty-six in the embittered mood of a struggling and hardly yet acknowledged dramatist. Twenty-seven years later, he returned as a European celebrity, indeed as one of the principal figures of modern literature. In

Christiania, where he settled for good, he became something of a national institution and was, evidently, far from disliking such a status. All the frustration and humiliation he had endured in youth and early manhood were now amply compensated for. He was not only a national, but a world figure. Nor was he a poor man any longer, for during his years of success he had shown amazing business acumen. He knew how to get every penny out of his publishers and where to invest it most profitably. He also timed the appearance of his plays in such a manner as to ensure good sales in advance. One of his expedients was to keep the public guessing and gossiping about each of his works for months before it appeared, and he never had any reason to regret such a method.

As if anxious to do full justice to his literary and social position, Ibsen now increased his air of excessively dignified respectability. So much so that in all his external habits he was, or pretended to be, even more strict and methodical than those philistines whom he had ridiculed with such stinging sarcasms in his works. Immaculately dressed in his frock-coat and silk top-hat, he took his daily walks along the same streets, sat at the same table in the same café (where all the customers respectfully rose whenever he entered), and went home at the same time—with the regularity of clockwork. He was also fond of displaying his numerous decorations, which he used to collect and covet with the relish of a *nouveau riche* enjoying all the external insignia of his own importance.

These peculiarities of Ibsen's character have been variously commented upon and still disturb many of his admirers. J. Paulsen, who happened to be one of his personal friends, says that however iconoclastic the great dramatist may have been in his writings, there still lingered quite a few bourgeois features in the hidden corners of his personality. 'In ordinary life he is extremely correct, conservative, and full of such pedantic respect for established conventions that any breach of external forms in communal life strikes him as offensive, even though excused by youth and lack of breeding. In his everyday existence he demands respect from that very bourgeoisie over which Ibsen the dramatist had pronounced sentence of death. He also pays the same respect to it, at least by observing all the outward formalities required.'

Paulsen compares the divergence between Ibsen's external and inner life with the case of Goethe, in whom—so he contends—the citizen and the personality had refused to merge. But in Ibsen's case the reasons have to be looked for elsewhere: above all in self-protection through polite aloofness and reserve; and then in a belated compensation for his early disappointments and feeling of social inferiority, which made him so embittered that he was reluctant to return—even as a man of sixty—to his native country. No sooner was he back, however, among the bourgeois who once had made him feel so 'small', than he may have found a secret pleasure in snubbing them, this time on their own ground—as a super-bourgeois (at least in appearance). Still, the private character of Ibsen matters to us only in so far as it helps us to elucidate the character of his work as a whole.

II

SOME ASPECTS OF IBSEN'S ART

I

WHATEVER the ultimate nature of art may be, the process of artistic creation always implies a conscious or unconscious reaction to life on the part of the creator himself. He either regards life and the world as something hostile to man, and adopts a negative attitude towards them; or else finds them worthy of acceptance in spite of all. In the first case, some sort of escapism (whether romantic, aesthetic, or otherwise), which by no means excludes a rancorous disparagement of reality, is the usual outcome. In the second case, however, the artist aims at an affirmation of life even if he is not quite sure about what exactly should be accepted and affirmed. The very lack of certainty may stimulate his quest, supported by a critical propensity which in this instance rejects only what deserves to be rejected, and may go hand in hand with a strong social or moral trend. This in turn often sidetracks even great creative minds away from art, the most warning example in recent times being that of Tolstoy.

Ibsen belongs—though not unconditionally—to the affirmative type. Even his romanticism was not of an escapist but of a militant kind, inspired by his yearning for a better man and a better world. This does not mean that Ibsen sacrificed the artistic side of his work to any moral, philosophic, or social considerations. In a way he balanced all these elements. The proportion between them varied, of course, according to his own needs and dispositions, which again were largely responsible for his choice of certain themes in preference to others. For all that, the artist and poet in him remained uppermost, even if his worship was devoted to truth rather than to beauty. In a letter he sent from Dresden to the Danish critic Brandes (July 1869) Ibsen made the characteristic statement that whereas the Southern artists endeavour to reach absolute beauty, to a Northerner even conventional ugliness may appear beautiful on account of the 'truth inherent in it'. He was and remained a typical Northerner in this respect—even during his prolonged stay in the south.

Another feature he never wearied of stressing was the individual factor, or self-expression in and through art. Unable to accept any conventional rules, cults, or canons for himself, he was always on his guard when he came across them in other people's work. Hence his lack of enthusiasm for ancient art, for example. On his arrival in Rome he felt more puzzled than elated by it, as one can conclude from these lines he wrote to Björnson on September 16th, 1864:

My mind has received many impressions, especially here in Rome. But I have not yet come to an understanding with ancient art; I cannot make out its connection with our own time. To me it lacks illusion, and above all, personal individual expression, both in the work of art and on the part of the artist; nor can I yet help often seeing only conventions where others maintain that there are enduring laws. . . . Michelangelo, and Bernini and his school, I understand better; those fellows had the courage to commit a folly occasionally.

Ibsen's indifference to ancient art, not only on account of its lack of individual flavour, but because he was unable to 'make out its connection with our own time', shows that his own individualism was of a peculiar stamp and had nothing to do with the 'ivory towers' of the romantics. Uprooted though he was socially, he strove to become the more alive to the spirit of the epoch to which he belonged. All the plays he wrote after his Bergen period are a proof of this. Never, not even during his most romantic phase, did Ibsen commit the *naïveté* of confusing artistic or aesthetic detachment with detachment from life, since life—sifted through individual experience—is the only vital source of any art that is worth while. But, if so, then a true artist has responsibilities with regard to life and must on no account run away from it. Ibsen's own emancipation from the aesthetic danger took place after he had left Norway, and the relief he felt is summed up in another letter to Björnson, dated September 12th, 1865, that is when he had been in Rome for more than a year:

If I were asked to tell at this moment, what exactly has been the chief result of my stay abroad, I should say that it consisted in my having driven out of myself the aestheticism which had a great power over me— an isolated aestheticism with a claim to independent existence. Aestheticism of this kind seems to me now as great a curse to poetry as theology is to religion. . . . Is it not an inexpressibly great gift of fortune to be able to write? But it brings with it great responsibility; and I am now sufficiently serious to realize this and to be very severe with myself. An aesthete in Copenhagen once said to me: 'Christ is really the most interesting phenomenon in world history.' The aesthete enjoyed him as the glutton does the sight of an oyster. I have always been too strong to become a creature of that type; but what the intellectual asses might have made of me if they had had me all to themselves, I know not.*

II

Only if we take this basic attitude of Ibsen for granted, can we proceed to some of those peculiarities of his creative process which were responsible for his plays being what they are. In his effort to seek and to find the truth inherent in the age in which he lived, Ibsen was one of those geniuses who create because they *must*. His work was conditioned by his own inner needs on the one hand, and by the *Zeitgeist* (the spirit of the age) on the other. Being in advance of the latter, he did not try to adjust himself to it, but rather to adjust it to himself, to his own demands and values. Hence the propensity to criticize and to reject which is so conspicuous in his art. His creative impetus seems to have been derived above all from his attitude of protest; not protest for its own sake, but for the sake of something better and worthier than the reality he was familiar with. All of which was fostered again by that basic inner urge which in each successive stage of his development looked for an outlet—the urge towards self-realization in the sense it was understood and interpreted by the most romantic individualist of that period, the Danish philosopher Sören Kierkegaard.

Surrounded by puzzles and riddles wherever he looked, Ibsen could not but brood all the more about the riddle of his own personality, of its destiny and meaning. This in turn led him to the question of what task, if any, he had to fulfil in the world: not a casual task, but that unconditional calling or vocation through which alone a man can fully justify his existence amidst the chaos of our ever-shifting dilemmas. Whatever the influence of Kierkegaard's philosophy on him may have amounted to, Ibsen was able to assimilate it only because it corresponded to certain propensities of his own. In any case, the problem of

* It is not surprising that characters with a leaning towards aestheticism are always depicted by Ibsen as shallow individuals: Einar in *Brand*; Helmer in *A Doll's House*; Hialmar in *The Wild Duck*.

2

self-realization crops up, in some form or other, in the majority of Ibsen's plays, and becomes of particular interest when intertwined with his moral sense or the sense of guilt which is so prominent in his works. He may express it in terms of 'gnawing conscience', of a coming retribution; but whatever its outward formula, it keeps recurring again and again. Ibsen's very idea of fate became in the end identical, or almost identical, with moral retribution. Imbued with a strong pietistic tradition, he thus retained his moral sense even after he had discarded his Christian convictions. His sense of guilt, as well as his fear of retribution, was all the stronger because he could not help being haunted by the memory of his illegitimate child, whom he had callously left to its own fate somewhere in the wilds of Norway. Even his continuous need to attack and to judge others may only have been an indirect way of attacking and judging himself, according to his well-known motto:

> At digte det er at holde
> Dommedag over sig selve.

> (To write poetry means to hold
> A judgment-day over oneself.)

But if Ibsen the man was weighed down by the burden of a 'gnawing conscience', Ibsen the artist provided a relief by projecting it into characters who, imaginary though they were, yet existed in their own right, that is, independently of Ibsen. He welcomed any pretext for an attack, because it was through fight and protest that he vented the moral indignation which otherwise might have turned against himself. His favourite attitude was that of a judge, critic and fighter in one, whose verbal indictments were the more virulent because of his timidity in practical life. Hence his instinctive search for things provocative even when the anger aroused by them was due to personal reasons. After some scathing reviews of his *Peer Gynt*, for instance, he wrote to Björnson in 1867:

I am glad of the injustice that has been done to me. There has been something of the God-sent, of the providential dispensation in it; for I feel that this anger is invigorating all my powers. . . . If it is to be war, then let it be war! If I am no poet, then I have nothing to lose. I shall try my luck as a photographer. My contemporaries in the North I shall take in hand one after the other. I will not spare the child in the mother's womb, nor the thought or the feeling that lies under the word of a living soul that deserves the honour of my notice.

His pugnacious temper is even better illustrated by this passage from a letter to Peter Hansen in 1870:

While writing *Brand*, I had on my desk a glass with a scorpion in it. From time to time the little animal was ill. Then I used to give it a piece of soft fruit, upon which it fell furiously and emptied its poison into it— after which it was well again. Does not something similar happen to us poets? The laws of nature regulate the spiritual world also. . . .

Translated into plain words: when feeling morally ill, Ibsen the poet would fall upon society and the age in order to empty the accumulated 'poison', after which he was probably well again— for a while. Feeding, like so many moderns, on negative stimuli, he could not do without foes. And the more objectionable the foe to be attacked, the better. Is it then surprising that, in spite of his reforming zeal, he welcomed or even postulated all sorts of adverse and ugly conditions on which he could feed both his wrath and his fighting spirit? When in 1870 Rome had been definitely freed, Ibsen complained of it in a letter to Brandes, and added: 'Yes—I must confess that the only thing I love about liberty is the struggle for it; I care nothing for the possession of it.' And again: 'He who possesses liberty otherwise than as a thing to be striven for, possesses it dead and soulless. So that a man who stops in the midst of the struggle and says, "Now I have it,"—thereby shows that he has lost it.'

Passages of this kind may, incidentally, shed some light on Ibsen's paradoxical conclusion that the liberals are liberty's worst enemies. Anxious to abolish those conditions in which people are compelled by their very indignation to fight and to die for freedom, they turn freedom itself into something static, especially where man's spirit is concerned. Hence 'freedom of thought and spirit thrives best under absolutism; this was shown in France, after-wards in Germany, and now in Russia'. He applied the same attitude to the fight for truth. Like Lessing before him, he regarded the striving for truth as being more important than the finding of it, since the dynamic tension of the quest and contest is always likely to summon the reserve of one's hidden strength. Such at any rate was one side of Ibsen's character, in which he resembled the hero of his early poem, *The Miner*. Imprisoned

in the 'mountain's living womb', the miner continues to hammer
his way through the dark underground even though his efforts may
not lead him out of it—may not lead him anywhere at all:

> Have I failed then? Does the way
> Lead not to the upper day?
> What though every hope be vain,
> Strike, my hammer, strike again.
>
> What though darkness be my lot,
> Strike, my hammer, falter not;
> What though every hope be vain,
> Strike, my hammer, strike again.
>
> (*Translated by R. A. Streatfield*)

The urge towards self-realization and all that is implied by it
was, however, powerful enough in Ibsen to save him from a mere
struggle for struggle's sake. It kept him on the look-out for aims,
ideas, and values worth fighting for. This again was fraught with
a considerable danger of tendentiousness which he managed to
avoid only because his artistic genius, instead of clashing with his
ethical propensities (as was the case with Tolstoy), actually
collaborated with them. Such collaboration was responsible for
quite a few original features of his work, notably for the part
played in it by 'ideas'. In this respect, too, Ibsen is a typical
representative of the modern drama as distinct from its old, and
especially its ancient, counterpart.

III

The ancient drama had its roots in the religious myth of the
collective consciousness. At its best it fostered and reflected the
deepest inner experience on the part of the entire community in
its contact with the mystery of life and the universe. Hence the
liturgical character of the Greek tragedy. Such a collective
approach to the universe by means of art has been left, however,
in the past. The modern mind in particular has replaced it by
a scientific and analytical attitude instead. Whereas Greek tragedy
experienced life from its centre, as it were, our modern drama
observes, judges, and analyses it from its periphery. Devoid of
that profound cosmic feeling which might serve as a unifying
factor from within, we tend to split up, to 'atomize' and disin-
tegrate everything we touch in the jungle of the rapidly increasing

new aspects and problems we are called to cope with. Instead of an integrating religious consciousness, we have at best its rationalistic substitute in the shape of a *Weltanschauung*, of 'ideas', with which we try to patch up the gaps in our perception of life as a whole only to be eventually landed in a succession of blindalleys, as was the case with Ibsen.

But before dealing with this aspect of his work, it is well worth examining the functions—technical or otherwise—of 'ideas' in Ibsen's art. This is indeed imperative in view of the fact that Ibsen's less sophisticated admirers often valued his plays not so much on account of their artistic side as because of the 'ideas' contained in them (most of which—if taken by themselves—look rather dated at present) and were inclined to interpret his work as either open or clandestine propaganda. Did not the feminists in the 'eighties and 'nineties claim the author of *A Doll's House* as the principal mouthpiece of their cause in European literature? Dr. Stockmann, the hero of *An Enemy of the People*, on the other hand, was hailed as an exponent of the views held by the individualists and anarchists. Even *Ghosts* was interpreted at the time as though it had been written not by Ibsen, but, say, by Brieux. All of which was, of course, misleading. Ibsen's 'ideas' are not those of a propagandist but of a seeker, who is on the look-out for the best artistic expression of the truth 'inherent' in life. They are also those of a fighter, anxious to undermine—not as a preacher but again as artist—the old dead values which still continue to encumber, like ghosts, our lives.

I almost think we are all of us ghosts [says Mrs. Alving in the play bearing the same title]. It is not only what we have inherited from our father and mother that 'walks' in us. It is all sorts of dead ideas, and lifeless old beliefs, and so forth. They have no vitality, but they cling to us all the same, and we cannot shake them off. Whenever I take up a newspaper, I see ghosts gliding between the lines. There must be ghosts all the country over, as thick as sands of the sea. And then we are, one and all, so pitifully afraid of the light.

It was 'ghosts' without and also those within himself that Ibsen fought to the bitter end. The phases of this struggle constitute his personal inner drama—the drama of his own conscience, which had its beginning, its heroic climax, and also its tragically inconclusive dénouement. Nothing could have been more determined or courageous than Brand's battle-call, voicing some of Ibsen's own moods and aspirations at the height of his manhood:

> Now but in shreds and scraps is dealt
> The Spirit we have faintly felt;
> But from these scraps and from these shreds,
> These headless hands and handless heads,
> These torso-stumps of soul and thought,
> A man complete and whole shall grow,
> And God His glorious child shall know,
> His heir, the Adam that He wrought.

But what a different tenor prevails in the last stage of Ibsen's career! While comparing his militant will with the moods of his later characters, especially of his camouflaged *alter ego*, the sculptor Rubek in *When We Dead Awaken*, one can obtain an idea of the price Ibsen had to pay for his quest and struggle. Rubek, too, like Brand and Ibsen himself, had started his vocation as a romantic idealist. His life-work was to be a statue of the Resurrection Day—in the shape of a 'young unsullied woman awakening to light and glory'. He dreamt in fact of remaking human beings through the magic of art, but the experiences he had to pass through taught him the bitter wisdom of knowledge.

I learned wisdom, Irene. The little round plinth on which your figure stood erect and solitary—it no longer afforded room for the imagery I now wanted to add. . . . I imagined that which I saw with my eyes around me in the world. I had to include it—I could not help it, Irene. I expanded the plinth—made it wide and spacious. And on it I placed a segment of the curving, bursting earth. And from the fissures of the soil there now swarm men and women with dimly suggested animal faces. Women and men as I knew them in real life.

Ibsen's own disappointment in 'ideas' and 'ideals' was hardly less acute as time went on. His dream of the Resurrection Day, that is of a renewal of man and life, had to be revised, and if not abandoned, at least indefinitely postponed. At the end of his fight and his quest, he was more baffled than ever and must have secretly smiled, many a time, at the eulogists of his art—in the way Rubek smiled at those who extolled the perfection of his busts and portraits, without suspecting the *arrière pensée* hidden behind their seeming perfection.

There is something equivocal, something cryptic, lurking in and behind these busts—a secret something that people cannot see . . . I alone can see it. And it amuses me unspeakably. On the surface I give them the 'striking likeness', as they call it, and they all stand in astonishment—but at the bottom they are all respectable, pompous horse-faces, and self-opinionated donkey-muzzles, and lop-eared, low-browed dog-skulls, and fatted swine-snouts, and sometimes dull, brutal bull-fronts as well.

Not a few of Ibsen's plays contain a 'secret something that people cannot see'. The gradual change which came over him from his middle period onwards was reflected mainly in the growth of that wistful anxiety with which he kept looking and wondering at the world at large, as well as at his own inner world. An idealist by nature, he was doomed to undermine, however reluctantly, his faith in one ideal after the other. His lips became tight, while his language grew increasingly laconic, cryptic, and also full of dashes—the language of one who is determined to be reticent about the things that could not be said to the end. As far as he said them at all, he now did it in symbols speaking of his 'vexation of the spirit'. Ibsen may have adopted, now and again, various positive aims to fight for. But in the long run his own intellectual honesty compelled him to take a sceptical view in the very teeth of his urges and wishes. Where once the statue of the Resurrection Day had stood in all its glory, there began to swarm 'men and women with dimly suggested animal faces. Women and men as I knew them in real life.'

Why is it that people who write about Ibsen always must resort to using his own phrases IV *to explain him, leaving the phrases unexplained?*

True enough, if one considers some of Ibsen's plays separately, that is out of context with the rest of his work, it is not difficult to prove that there were times when he seemed to be on the verge of championing certain trends or ideas. More reflective than imaginative, he could not help conceiving many of his plays in terms of reasoned-out statements. Among his notes for *A Doll's House*, for example, one can read passages such as these:

There are two kinds of spiritual law, two kinds of conscience—one in man and another, altogether different, in woman. They do not understand each other; but in practical life the woman is judged by man's law, as though she were not a woman but a man. . . . Woman cannot be herself in the society of the present day, which is exclusively masculine society, with the laws framed by men and with a judicial system that judges feminine conduct from a masculine point of view. . . . A mother in modern society is like certain insects who go away and die when they have done their duty in the propagation of the race.

Or take Ibsen's jottings for *Ghosts* (the range of which is wider).

Marriage for external reasons, even when these are religious and moral, brings a Nemesis upon the offspring. . . . These women of the present day, ill used as daughters, as sisters, as wives, not educated according to their gifts, prevented from following their inclination, deprived of their inheritance, embittered in temper—it is these who furnish the mothers of the new generation. What is the result? The keynote is to be: The prolific growth of our intellectual life, in literature, art, etc.—and in contrast to this: the whole of mankind gone astray. . . . Among us monuments are erected to the dead, since we have a duty towards them; we allow lepers to marry, but their offspring—? The unborn—?

Even more tantalizing are Ibsen's notes (with a bearing upon atavism, adjustment, and the Unconscious) in his *The Lady from the Sea*:

Has the line of human development gone astray? Why have we come to belong to the dry land? Why not to the air? Why not to the sea? The longing to possess wings. The strange dreams that one can fly without being surprised at it—how is all this to be interpreted? . . . Human beings akin to the sea. Dependent on the sea. Compelled to return to it. A fish species forms a primitive link in the chain of evolution. Are rudiments thereof still present in the human mind? In the mind of certain individuals? . . . The sea possesses a power over one's moods that has the effect of a will. The sea can hypnotize. Nature in general can do so. The great mystery is the dependence of the human will on that which is will-less.

From musings of this kind one would expect didactic essays and treatises rather than plays. Yet instead of pamphlets on feminine mentality, the nature of marriage, or the unnerving influence of the sea, Ibsen presented the world with such creations as Nora Helmer, Oswald and Mrs. Alving, and the morbidly maladjusted wife Ellida Wangel—all of them as clear-cut and concrete as they could be. Nor are his plays cleverly dramatized lectures with the author standing behind and pulling the wires: his characters, even when voicing his own views, exist independently of him. Ideas are not imposed upon—they are *embodied* in them. Instead of puppets, we see on the stage people of flesh and blood, each of whom has his own face, his own voice and destiny.

Ibsen was fully aware of the difference between such embodied ideas and those merely pasted upon ready-made figures for the sake of a 'purpose', or of propaganda in general. Even apropos of his most intellectual drama, *Emperor and Galilean*, he warned Brandes not to expect any 'tendency nonsense', and added by way of explanation: 'I look at the characters, at the conflicting designs, at history, and do not concern myself with the moral of it at all. Of course, you will not confound the moral of history with its philosophy; for that must inevitably shine forth as the final verdict of the conflicting and the conquering forces.' No 'tendency nonsense' in the strict sense of this word can be extracted from *A Doll's House* either, however vociferously it was acclaimed by the suffragettes as a Magna Charta of feminism. In all the noise of this kind Ibsen only saw a series of misunderstandings. We have his own word for it. When at a festival in 1898 the Norwegian Women's Rights League welcomed him as a champion of feminist movement, he gave this enlightening if rather blunt answer:

I am not a member of the Women's Rights League. Whatever I have written, has been without any conscious thought of making propaganda. I have been more poet and less social philosopher than people generally seem inclined to believe. I thank you for the toast, but must disclaim the honour of having consciously worked for the Women's Rights Movement. I am not quite clear as to just what the Women's Rights Movement really is. And if you read my books carefully, you will understand this. True enough, it is desirable to solve the problem of Women's Rights along with the others; but that has not been the whole purpose. My task has been the description of humanity.

V

What Ibsen says of *A Doll's House* holds good of his other works as well, even of those which are crammed with 'ideas'. This is the more remarkable because the preliminary notes, drafts and sketches of his dramas amply testify to the laborious process,

as well as to the resistance on the part of the material he had to
overcome, while thus transposing 'ideas' into works of art, i.e.
expressing them in terms of living characters and dramatic
action. The process was by no means a quick one. Most of his
later plays took two years each to complete. On the other hand
the method he used gave him an artistic tact and discipline the
equal of which is not easy to find. He was endowed, moreover,
with an architectonic sense by virtue of which he could strip his
material down to mere essentials without ever making it look bald
or barren. It was a hard struggle (he wrote several drafts for each
of his plays), but he never paused until he achieved a maximum
of economy and concentration. We would look in vain for any
padding even in his early works. His characters are so organically
intertwined with the structure, with the happenings and the
phases of the plot, that no margin is left for anything superfluous
or casual.

The same tightness marks his dialogue. Each of his repartees
is in its proper place, and in his later works there is no room for
either soliloquies or asides, both of which seemed to him un-
natural. Ibsen was no less particular about the names of his
characters. These he kept changing a number of times (five times
in the case of Rosmer) before he was satisfied. It is true that
quite a few of his characters were shaped under the auspices of
some 'idea'; but even so, we remember them only as characters
and not as abstract ideas. He is also a past master in blending
the most contradicting ingredients, calculated to increase the
effect of a scene: pathos mixed with humour; tragedy with
satire; preaching with parody. Because of such calculation
the Norwegian author Knut Hamsun once referred—rather con-
temptuously—to Ibsen as a book-keeper of dramatic art. Björnson,
too, said that Ibsen was not a man but only a pen. Some German
critics have called his self-conscious creative process *Verstandes-
dramatik* (intellectual dramatic art), which may sound more like
a reproach than a compliment. And if it is a reproach, it certainly
does not quite tally with the strong irrational element in *Brand*,
Rosmersholm, *The Lady from the Sea*, and especially in *The Master
Builder*. Nor should one overlook the fact that Ibsen's incredible
'book-keeping' cannot be separated from his innovations in the
modern drama; from that intensive and essentially 'vertical' type
of play for which he is largely responsible.

Having learned what he could from Scribe, from Hettner's book, from Friedrich Hebbel, from the Greek tragedies (those of Sophocles in particular), and perhaps also from Racine, Ibsen proceeded to the creation of his own type of play which is really a dramatic development of the catastrophe and not of the plot in the old sense. The misdeed of the hero does not take place on the stage as was the case with the traditional drama, but is relegated to the past. What we see are the inevitable consequences, the 'retribution', following upon the crime—as in the *Oresteia*, for instance, but worked out in Ibsen's manner. Such a departure from tradition led, however, to several structural peculiarities of the so-called Ibsenian drama. The first play in which Ibsen made full use of his retrospective exposition of the hero's guilt was *The Vikings in Helgeland*. But here he still balanced the inner tension with a fairly rich external action. In his later plays, however, action in the old sense was more and more replaced by tension of a mental or psychological order, and by dialogue manipulated in such a way as to reveal, analytically and step by step, all the implications of the hero's or heroine's past. This again required a new type of acting in which the voice, the inflection, the pauses, the smallest gestures and psychological 'imponderables' played a much greater part than in the pre-Ibsenian drama.

Whereas external action as such thus tended to be more or less static, the dialogue became increasingly dynamic, as well as full of subtle hints and allusions. Ibsen's capacity for conveying unspoken thought, together with all its emotional and mental undercurrents, is often uncanny. So is the manner in which he reconstructs the past guilt of his hero, while at the same time conjuring up an atmosphere charged with retribution that comes not from without but from within. His drama at its most typical passes into a drama of conscience, and its dénouement usually coincides with a radical inner change undergone by the character concerned. Consul Bernick in *The Pillars of Society*, Nora in *A Doll's House*, Rebecca in *Rosmersholm*, Solness in *The Master Builder*, Rita and Alfred Allmers in *Little Eyolf*, Rubek in *When We Dead Awaken*—they all perceive in and through their crisis some inner truth which makes them see everything, including themselves, in a new light. The effect is often accompanied by a confession which Ibsen uses, in the case of Bernick, Rebecca,

Solness and Rubek, as an essential part of the climax. All this is strengthened by Ibsen's skill in dramatic suspense. He knows how to interrupt an act, or a scene, just at the right moment in order to whet the curiosity of the spectators—a tension which is enhanced by his frequent observance of the unity of time. Most of his plays after *Emperor and Galilean* last less than three days. In *Ghosts* and *The Wild Duck* this unity is almost complete, whereas in *John Gabriel Borkman* there is no lapse of time between the acts.

VI

One of Ibsen's sayings is, 'To be a poet one must see', and it is truly remarkable to what extent he saw his characters—down to the shape of their hands. They are always palpable and real personalities. A number of them are based—so it seems —on his own acquaintances, whose individual features he often stressed, intensified, or modified, according to the requirements of the part. Brand, for instance, may have been modelled on Pastor Lammers. The model for Aase in *Peer Gynt* was— with 'unavoidable exaggerations'—Ibsen's own mother, whereas old Ekdal in *The Wild Duck* is supposed to be a portrait of Ibsen's bankrupt father gone to seed. Johannes Rosmer in *Rosmersholm* shows several traits of Ibsen's Swedish friend, the poet Count Carl Snoilsky. Ellida in *The Lady from the Sea* is a more composite character: with a few features taken from the Norwegian authoress Camilla Collett, and others from Ibsen's mother-in-law Magdalene Thoresen. The wayward genius Lövborg again (in *Hedda Gabler*) portrays the brilliant Danish philologist Julius Hoffory, who was Professor in Berlin and through his dissipations came to an untimely death.

The list could be extended. What strikes one is not only the visual concreteness of Ibsen's characters, but also the way they complete one another in so calculated a manner that they form a pattern as perfect in this respect as the pattern of Turgenev's novels. Another striking characteristic of Ibsen's work as a whole is the relative paucity of themes he makes use of. Instead of enlarging their number, he prefers to tackle the same or similar themes and situations again and again—each time from a different angle. The frequency of the main hero wavering between two women, for example, is most conspicuous in his plays. So is the invariable repetition of some of his basic characters. The two contrasted women, Furia and Aurelia, in his first play (*Catilina*) can actually be traced throughout the whole of his work: from Hjördis and Dagny in *The Vikings in Helgeland* to Hedda and Thea in *Hedda Gabler*, or to Mrs. Borkman and her sister Ella in *John Gabriel Borkman*. Even when not contrasted in one and the same play, Ibsen's women as a rule belong to one or the other of these two types: the self-reliant, aggressive and often destructive 'Valkyrie' on the one hand, and her devoted, self-sacrificing opposite (such as Agnes in *Brand*, Solveig in *Peer Gynt*, and Margerita in *The Pretenders*) on the other. In Rebecca (*Rosmersholm*) again one can see the transition from the first to the second type—a transition motivated both morally and psychologically as only Ibsen was able to do it.

Needless to say, a drama based principally on the so-called inner action as expressed through the dialogue must impart to the dialogue itself a new dimension as it were—by deepening it into that parallel inner dialogue 'between the lines', which often fills the simplest words and remarks with a second meaning. Take the commonplace yet so ominous last words exchanged between Nora and Rank after the Christmas party in *A Doll's House*; the last scene between Ulrik Brendel, Rebecca, and Rosmer in *Rosmersholm*; or most of the conversation between Solness and Hilda in *The Master Builder*. Ibsen knows, moreover, how to envelop the realism of his plays in a symbolic aura, the cumulative effect of which can only be rendered by adequate acting. His deliberate and calculated symbols, on the other hand, are not always successful. The high tower in *The Master Builder*, or the ascent of the mountain (with the subsequent avalanche) in *When We Dead Awaken*, is nearer to a cliché or a trite allegory than to a symbol. Even in his masterpiece, *Peer Gynt*, there are a few pseudo-symbols which, instead of explaining themselves, are in need of explanatory footnotes and comments.

This deficiency is, however, amply compensated by the already mentioned symbolic flavour of Ibsen's realism, and particularly by the skill with which he shows the ordinary Norwegian provincials, with their musings, conflicts, and dilemmas, in a broad universal perspective. No less important is the cathartic nature of his plays—written under the pressure of inner experience, of *Erlebnis*, which found its natural sublimation in art. To quote a passage from Ibsen's letter to his German translator L. Passarge: 'Everything I have written has the closest possible connection with what I lived through, even if that has not been my personal —or actual—experience. I have aimed in every poem or play at my own spiritual emancipation and purification—for a man shares the responsibility and the guilt of the age he belongs to.' Which brings us to some further peculiarities of his work.

VII

One of these is the strange interdependence between Ibsen's plays. Each theme tackled by him seems to have grown out of a previous one as its natural amplification and clarification, but always against the background of some fundamental problem, or problems, of life. He thus throve best at the cross-roads where art and ethics meet. Yet whatever he wrote bore the stamp of his militant individualism which, ethical though it may have been in its essence, often verged on the egotistic exclusiveness recommended by him (in a letter) to Brandes: 'What I chiefly desire for you is a genuine full-blooded egoism which, for a time, will force you to regard yourself as the only thing of any consequence and everything else as non-existent.'

In Ibsen's case, such an attitude was one of self-assertion against the outside world and also self-defence against his own doubts of himself. While challenging both, he gathered the necessary strength which, for reasons of his own, he hoped best to preserve by 'standing alone'. Hence it would be futile to look to him for expansiveness, for any signs of overflowing warmth and sympathy. Unable to absolve, he was yet always ready to judge and to condemn, especially when prompted by his moral indignation. But a strong moral sense, if not counterbalanced by an adequate religious sense (with all the sympathy it implies), can easily lead to exaggerated self-righteousness and to that moral solipsism which Ibsen projected into his Brand, for instance.

Ibsen's personal tragedy was due to his incurably idealistic temperament—confronted by a cold analytical mind which, feeding too much on his own exclusiveness, in the end threatened to destroy and almost succeeded in destroying his faith in any ideas or ideals. For the sceptic in him took the upper hand at a time when he himself could least afford an issue amounting to an open or veiled defeat. Ibsen the dramatist thus provides a sufficient illustration of the inner spiritual drama of Ibsen the man, and vice versa. But if he wrote about things which had the 'closest possible connection' with what he had lived through, he also distilled those experiences into plays which remain the pride and the glory of European literature as a whole.

III

A ROMANTIC REBEL

I

IBSEN'S first dramatic venture, *Catilina*, reflected the political and social situation in Europe of 1848, as seen through the spectacles of a rebellious pharmacy assistant at Grimstad. Years later—in October 1870—he said in a letter to Peter Hansen that *Catilina* had been written in a 'little provincial town, where it was impossible to give expression to all that fermented in my mind except by mad, riotous pranks, which brought down upon me the ill-will of all respectable citizens, who could not enter into that world which I was wrestling with alone'. The very subject chosen by Ibsen was significant. While preparing for his examination, he became interested in Sallust's panorama of decayed Roman society and also in Cicero's diatribes against Catilina. It did not take long for him to discover analogies between the decadence of the Romans and his own period. And as for Cicero's scapegoat Catilina, he at once recognized in him a kindred spirit, into whom he could safely project some of his own revolutionary moods and tendencies. 'Catilina *versus* Rome' became a transposition of Ibsen *versus* the philistine society in the year of grace 1848. It was therefore natural for the author to endow him with several characteristics of his own, such as his fierce individualism, for example, or his brooding 'nocturnal' disposition—practically the entire action takes place at night-time. Like Ibsen, Catilina, too, suffers from an inner split (illustrated by his wavering between Furia and Aurelia). Even Catilina's desire to shake the dust of Rome off his feet and to emigrate to some distant region of the Empire seems to reflect Ibsen's smouldering wish to escape from Norway and to settle abroad, whatever the price.

Technically, the play is juvenile and groping. Its blank verse (the five-footed iambic) is far from being perfect, and the same can be said about the structure in general. Yet in his preface to the second edition (1875) of *Catilina* Ibsen himself remarked with justice that several elements of his later dramas were anticipated in this work. He pointed out above all the 'contrast between one's abilities and one's ambitions; between what one wills and what one can actually achieve—a clash constituting the tragedy as well as the comedy of the individual'. Even Ibsen's basic theme—that of self-realization through one's destined task or calling—is vaguely suggested in it, not to speak of his concentration on the inner conflict, as well as the transference of the hero's guilt (Catilina's seduction of Aurelia) into the past.

After the disappointment *Catilina* had brought him, Ibsen decided to strike a different note in his next work—the one-act play in verse, *The Warriors' Mound*, in which he evidently made a concession to the current fashion. His hope that the play might appeal to the public was soon justified, although its success on the stage of the Christiania theatre was due to its conventionality rather than to any particular artistic merits. This time it was not rebellion, but the Viking romanticism in the popular taste that proved decisive. Ibsen took his operatic Vikings as far as Sicily, where their paganism was suddenly confronted by the new Christian religion of mercy—embodied in the expatriated hermit Roderick and in his adopted daughter Blanca (echoes of Prospero and Miranda). There is little or no psychological motivation in this work, which otherwise can serve as a prelude to Ibsen's Bergen period.

II

The principal characteristics of that period coincided with the national-patriotic as well as folkloristic trend in Scandinavian, and more particularly Norwegian, romanticism. Strangely enough, the six or seven years of Ibsen's adherence to it opened with one of his weakest plays, *St. John's Night*, and ended with the hardly more remarkable *Olaf Liljenkrans*, both of them written in verse and inspired by Norwegian folk-songs and folk-ballads. The second of them even retains the same title as the ballad from which it was derived.* Fortunately, his years of apprenticeship at Bergen were not limited to this kind only. In such plays as *Lady Inger of Östraat*, *The Feast of Solhoug*, and *The Vikings in Helgeland* he branched off in other directions, while still keeping to the prevalent romantic genre.

Lady Inger of Östraat (written, according to Ibsen, as the 'result

* Another influence was the folk-tale *Justendalsrypa* (*the Partridge of Justendal*). As early as 1850, Ibsen jotted down two acts of a play, *The Partridge*, Astfield (as in *Olaf Liljenkrans*) being its heroine.

of a love-affair—hastily entered into and violently broken off') is, amongst other things, also a historical play. So it is of no small interest to watch how Ibsen modified history and the characters in order to adjust them to the requirements of his art. For one thing, this drama is compact in spite of its length, and the unity of time is so severely preserved that all its five acts take place in one single night. Here for the first time Ibsen handled the dramatic moments with perfect self-assurance, but at the expense of historical truth. Although the events he deals with actually happened in 1528, the principal details of the play are a product of Ibsen's own imagination. Neither the conflict between patriotism and personal love in Elina, nor the battle of wits and cunning between Lady Inger and the Danish diplomat Nils Lykke is true to history. The real Lady Inger was not such a high-minded idealist thinking only of Norway's salvation as Ibsen would have it. Her supposed son (whom, in the play, she sacrifices to her patriotism) was also an invention, but from a dramatic standpoint quite an effective one. The same applies to the character of Nils Lykke. Yet however much it diverges from history, the play remains poetically true and convincing. It proves above all that meanwhile Ibsen had learned a great deal about dramatic technique and was beginning to make use of it.

As for *The Feast of Solhoug* (written in verse and in prose), Ibsen did not rate it very highly and called it a lyrical drama. It deals with the past, but its subject-matter, as well as the treatment, seems to be nearer to an opera than to a play. Still, even if we look at it as a kind of anticlimax after *Lady Inger of Östraat*, Ibsen's art of portraiture in a convincing three-dimensional manner comes out here to the best advantage. The good-natured, trustful and rather stupid Bengt (an anticipation of Jörgen Tesman in *Hedda Gabler*) and his masterful wife Margit are a proof. In addition, the author broached this time one of his favourite problems—the maladjusted marriage.

Masterly characterizations, combined with surprising dramatic effects, are to be found, however, in *The Vikings in Helgeland*. The play is based on the Icelandic *Völsunga Saga*, which Ibsen knew from N. N. Petersen's translation. Its figures are presented on a legendary heroic scale even if the main theme—the betrayal of a devoted woman's love and its fatal consequences—is an eternal one and therefore topical at any age. Ibsen, who for some hidden reasons of his own, repeated this theme in a number of plays, depicts here the vengeance of Hjördis, the love for whom Sigurd had sacrificed to his friendship for Gunnar, thereby committing a crime against life itself. 'All good gifts may a man give his faithful friend—all save the woman he loves; for if he do that, he rends the Norn's secret web, and two lives are wrecked,' Hjördis reproaches him many years later, while already serving as an instrument of vengeance and retribution. Although the same subject-matter has been treated, apart from Ibsen, by Friedrich Hebbel (who took it from the *Nibelungenlied*) and Richard Wagner, Ibsen's dramatic version holds its own not only by its compactness of composition, but also by its incredibly terse dialogue. It is the more regrettable that the play is written in an over-stylized prose, the archaisms of which may not appeal to a modern listener or reader.

Besides, Ibsen must have felt by then somewhat weary of dealing with the past. The weakness of *Olaf Liljenkrans* (the last product of his Bergen period) was a sign that the dramatist in him needed a new and different focus. After all, he was a fighter, and who is going to fight in the name of things that are dead or legendary? Why not turn to the throbbing present instead? To the themes and motifs vitally important for his own age? A change of this kind took place in him soon after his departure to Christiania in 1859, as one can see from his *Love's Comedy*.

III

This work is first of all a romantic attack on marriage, but not in the spirit of a mere *épatez le bourgeois*. Ibsen tried to go deeper than that by probing the fundamental relationship between love and marriage—even if his approach may have been prompted by a foregone paradoxical conclusion. Is marriage as the institution we know, compatible with love at all? Or is it perhaps but a conventional lie which ought to be exposed without mercy in order to save love in its creative sense? Ibsen, who had a son born out of marriage, was only too glad to undermine the glamour of holy wedlock and to proclaim it a negation rather than the crowning glory of love. It needed a great deal of courage in those days to debunk all the cant about 'married bliss'; and it was Ibsen's mouthpiece, the poet Falk, who reared the battle flag of defiance.

> Yes, it is war I mean with nail and tooth
> Against the lie with the tenacious root,
> The lie that you have fostered into fruit,
> For all its strutting in the guise of truth.

Ibsen does not shrink from declaring, and most emphatically, that marriage is the tomb not only of love, but also of those higher aims and aspirations in the name of which an individual could be true to himself. The question arises what exactly made him attack marriage with such violence at a time when he himself was quite happily married. The only answer is that in doing this he found a safeguard against the usual dangers of married life—beset by poverty, by worries about daily bread, and by the temptations to make all sorts of compromises for the sake of a good income and the usual bourgeois comfort. The play was an act of inner emancipation. Ibsen himself said as much, when confessing in a letter to Clemens Petersen:

I can assure you that if ever it was necessary for an author to rid himself of a sentiment and a subject, it was so with me when I began that work. . . . Not until I was married did more serious interests take possession of my life. The first outcome of this change was a long poem, *Paa Vidderne* (*On the Heights*). The desire for emancipation which pervades this poem did not, however, receive its full expression until I wrote *Love's Comedy*, a book which gave rise to much talk in Norway. People mixed up my personal affairs in the discussion, and I fell greatly in the public esteem. The only person at that time who approved of the book was my wife. Hers is exactly a character desiderated by a man of mind—she is illogical, but has a strong poetic instinct, a broad and liberal mind, and an almost violent antipathy to all petty considerations. All this my countrymen did not understand, and I did not choose to make them my father-confessors. So they excommunicated me. All were against me.

There are three protagonists in this play: the poet Falk, his sweetheart Svanhild, and the solid matter-of-fact realist and merchant Guldstad. The background is provided by a number of engaged, married, and shortly-to-be-married couples, with the mammas and aunties keeping an eye on the 'one thing needful'. As a paragon of married happiness Pastor Strawman is paraded before us: once an active and even adventurous idealist, but now only a shell of a human being, always followed by his spouse and his eight daughters—with another four at home and another arrival in prospect. But among the engaged couples, too, the same spirit seems to be at work already. Prospective careers, salaries, and other blessings essential for a 'happy' married existence are not a joking matter, after all. The pity of it is, however, that their very touch seems to be fatal to love, especially when nourished by the atmosphere of suburban gossip, inquisitive envy, and the scramble for daily bread.

When Falk and Svanhild meet and fall in love with each other, they both instinctively protest against the degradation of marriage they see around. The actual and potential Strawmanism fills them not only with disgust, but with a determination to show through personal example what true marriage—marriage as a vehicle towards self-realization—could and should be like. Falk wants to realize himself through it as a poet, whereas Svanhild sees her own destiny in keeping his creative glow alive by warding off all the mean and petty elements of married existence.

> O, Svanhild, let us battle side by side!
> Thou fresh glad blossom flowering by the tomb,—
> See what the life is that they call youth's bloom!
> There's coffin-stench of bridegroom and of bride;
> There's coffin-stench wherever two go by
> At the street corner, smiling outwardly—
> With falsehood's reeking sepulchre beneath,
> And in their blood the apathy of death.
> And this they think is living! Heaven and earth,
> Is such a load so many antics worth?
> For such an end to haul up babes in shoals,
> To pamper them with honesty and reason,
> To feed them fat with faith one sorry season,
> For service, after killing-day, as souls.

Their dream of an ideal married union, so different from others, is undermined, however, by the practical world-wise Guldstad.

> He came with worldly cunning, stole our faith,
> Sowed doubt, and all the glory pass'd away!

Guldstad, too, wants to marry Svanhild and fights for her hand, but in his own manner. Knowing not only the value but also the price of things, he sets out to destroy the engagement between Falk and Svanhild by first destroying their illusion that marriage and love can be identical, or at least compatible. And in this he succeeds. Even without over-stressing the ominous side of the wedded bliss as represented by the Pastor and his progeny, Guldstad gradually makes the two lovers aware of the fact that any marriage is bound to turn sooner or later against love and to become its tomb. He frankly confesses to them that he himself aspires to Svanhild's hand, but that he knows what he is doing. It is not love he is after. The maximum that he hopes to get out of marriage is mutual esteem, companionship, and tolerance, supported, of course, by the wealth at his disposal—hardly a negligible factor in this world of ours. He is tactful enough to give Svanhild complete freedom of choice between Falk and himself. In case she should choose Falk he, moreover, promises to make both of them his sole heirs.

Falk is aghast when listening to Guldstad's cold and politely cynical arguments. Svanhild, too, is at first reluctant to agree with what he says. Gradually, however, she sees from the living examples around only too well how right Guldstad is. As a result she finds herself in the dilemma of choosing between love and marriage. Paradoxically, she chooses both, but only by separating them. She does not waver in her love for Falk, yet she cancels her decision to become his wife. She cancels it at the very climax of their mutual affection, and does not mind the prospect of becoming Guldstad's wife, provided the love she had kindled in Falk's heart remains intact. Falk, too, in the end accepts his lot and even finds in the grief engendered through his sacrifice a new source of inspiration. Since marriage and love seem to be incompatible, he sides with love in what he regards as its most creative aspect.

> Now I divine!
> Thus and not otherwise canst thou be mine!
> As the grave opens into Life's Dawn-fire,
> So Love with Life may not espoused be
> Till, loosed from longing and from wild desire,
> It soars into the heaven of memory.

SVANHILD (*in rapture*):

> My task is done!
> Now I have filled thy soul with song and sun.
> Forth! Now thou soarest on triumphant wings—
> Forth! Now thy Svanhild is the swan that sings!

FALK (*firmly*):

> And now to day's duties, each, alone.
> Our paths no more will mingle. Each must wage
> His warfare single-handed, without moan.
>
> Yes, upward is my flight; the winged steed
> Is saddled; I am strung for noble deed.
> And now, farewell!

IV

The motif of sacrifice, worked out in Ibsen's poem *On the Heights*, thus comes here into its own. So does that of self-realization through one's appointed calling—in the spirit of Sören Kierkegaard, who (like Falk) had given up his fiancée, Regine Olsen, in order to be entirely free for his 'great task'. *Love's Comedy* is in fact the first work in which Kierkegaard's influence on Ibsen is noticeable beyond any doubt. One is inclined to interpret some of Ibsen's passages, in spite of all the differences, as an adaptation from *The Diary of the Seducer*. The hero, analysed by Kierkegaard in this particular work, is an aesthetic voluptuary who is on the look-out for a fleeting love in order to intensify his own emotions, which are of course on a plane different from that of Falk's, yet reveal some curious external coincidences. This is how the Seducer reasons when in love with Cordelia:

> I am an aesthete, an eroticist, one who has understood the nature and meaning of love and knows it from the ground up, and only makes the private reservation that no love-affair should last more than six months at the most, and that every erotic relationship should cease as soon as one has had the ultimate enjoyment. I know all this, I know too that the highest conceivable enjoyment lies in being loved; to be loved is higher than anything in the world.
>
> When I have brought her to the point where she has learned what it is to love, and what it is to love me, then the engagement breaks like an imperfect mould, and she belongs to me. This is the point at which others become engaged and have a good prospect of a boring marriage for all eternity. Well, let others have it. . . .

Even had he first intended to portray in Falk such an aesthetic type as a contrast to philistines in love, Ibsen was too much of a moralist and puritan by instinct to treat him from such an angle. Besides, the Seducer was meant by Kierkegaard as a

warning; so he analysed him from that ethical ground which he
himself had in common with Ibsen. In his Falk-Svanhild motif,
Ibsen transposed the Seducer's short-lived aesthetic raptures of
love to a deeper dimension, in which love, instead of being a
sterile aesthetic pleasure, is expected to remain man's creative
inspiration to the end of his days.

   Love's Comedy is the most biting and ironical of Ibsen's early
works. This does not mean, however, that it is without snags.
There are quite a few of them, beginning with the question of
whether Falk and Svanhild had not unwittingly chosen the line
of least resistance. After all, if marriage is such a danger to love,
then would it not have been a braver deed on their part to face
marriage itself for the sake of love and make it truly worth while
rather than run away from it? Another problem: how far was
Falk morally entitled to accept Svanhild's sacrifice for the sake
of his own poetic self-realization? Was there nothing in her that
deserved to be equally developed and realized? Had she any right
to turn herself only into a means for the sake of another person's
'great task', in spite of the sincere love which prompted her to
do this? A debatable point is also Svanhild's decision to marry
Guldstad. Since she had come to the conclusion that marriage
was a degrading institution, why did she not keep entirely out of
it instead of giving her hand to a rich wooer, whom she did not
even love? How easily could such a dénouement be interpreted
as a *mariage de convenance* in the most pedestrian bourgeois style!
Ibsen once said in a private conversation that any thought carried
to the end usually touches upon its own contradiction, but in this
case the contradiction is dangerously close to parody.

   From a purely dramatic angle the principal weakness of *Love's
Comedy* lies, obviously, in the fact that the much too sudden change
of Svanhild and Falk is due not to an actual inner crisis, but to
the reasoned-out arguments, marshalled by the 'worldly cunning'
of Guldstad—a bourgeois himself, and a bourgeois by conviction.
Imagine two 'superior' human beings making the most fateful
decision in their lives because of a few arguments on the part
of a benevolent philistine whose philosophy of life is of no
particular interest to either. But though such considerations may
diminish the value of the play, the blows Ibsen delivered in it
retain much of their initial fury. He was now out for a fight,
and when fighting he spared neither friend nor foe. Soon,

however, he gave a proof of what he could achieve as a dramatist pure and simple in *The Pretenders*—the greatest play that came from his pen before he left Scandinavia.

V

In *The Pretenders* Ibsen took up Norwegian history once again, but with a difference. This time he used the events of the past chiefly as a pretext for exploring through the dramatic conflicts and characters certain aspects of his main dilemma: that of self-realization. Although the play is full of incidents and movement, its core lies in the inner contrast between King Haakon—the man with a life-task, and his opponent, Earl Skule, who is devoid of such a task. It matters little whether or not King Haakon is true to history. Even his 'great idea' of turning the Norwegian State into a Norwegian nation is less important in itself than as an aim which dominates the whole of his life and becomes in fact his destiny. Being a man of *ingenium*, chosen by Fate to accomplish big things, he never wavers in the knowledge of his calling. As his ambitions transcend his own self, he acts like the medium of some higher power from which he derives all his strength. This is why he invariably marches towards the goal with the self-confidence of one of the elect.

Quite a different character is his opponent, Earl Skule. He, too, is a strong man like Haakon, but his strength is not guided by a calling or a 'great idea' through the service of which he could realize himself; so he has none of Haakon's faith in himself. His deeds and actions are dictated by personal ambitions; and the more he is immersed in his own personality, the less he is able to rid himself of doubt and vacillation. Like Hamlet, he broods and waits until he has missed all his opportunities. In contrast to the always successful Haakon, he is only 'God's stepson on earth'. Luck is never on his side, and his life is one long failure.

There is yet a third colossal and truly Shakespearian figure in this play: Bishop Nicholas. Antagonistic to Haakon and to Earl Skule, he is more complicated than either. His dominant passion is lust for power. But as he is aware of his own mediocrity, his insatiable vainglory turns him into a moral cripple—possessed by something like demoniac mania to frustrate everybody and everything that has any promise of greatness or success. He plays the part of an evil genius in the fate of King Haakon, and also in

that of Earl Skule, whose doom is accelerated through the
Bishop's intervention. The sole pleasure he can still derive from
life is that of destruction. Even after his death he seems to hover,
like a shadow or a horrid spectre, over the events of history—
threatening to contaminate all that harbours any germs of good.

The disturbing problem of one's life-task, as well as the gap
between one's capacity and one's ambitions, was illustrated by
Ibsen in the three characters mentioned at a time when he, too,
was still struggling both for faith in himself and for a belated
recognition of his literary achievements. Hardly acknowledged
as yet by his contemporaries, he must often have felt doubts of
his talent and calling, like the hesitant Earl Skule. The Haakon
element, on the other hand, was more typical of his rival Björnson,
who always knew what he wanted and went straight to his goal.
This brief dialogue between Earl Skule and the skald Jatgeir is
suggestive also of the contrast between Ibsen and Björnson—as
seen through the eyes of the doubting Ibsen.

'Tell me, Jatgeir, how came you to be a skald? Who taught you
skaldcraft?'
'Skaldcraft cannot be taught, my lord.'
'Cannot be taught? How came it then?'
'The gift of sorrow came to me, and I was a skald.'
'Then 'tis the need of sorrow that a skald has need of?'
'I needed sorrow; others may be who need faith or joy—or doubt—'
'Doubt as well?'
'Ay; but then must the doubter be strong and sound.'
'And whom do you call the unsound doubter?'
'He who doubts his own doubt.'
'That, methinks, were death.'
' 'Tis worse, 'tis neither day nor night.'

To all of which Earl Skule slowly replies:

'Where are my weapons? I will fight and act—not think.'

Ibsen, too, like Earl Skule, decided to fight in all earnest, and
his plays (and occasional poems) remained his principal, his only
weapons. This task was made easier for him once he had left
for Italy, whence he could scrutinize his own countrymen in
terms of broader perspectives and vistas. The first result of such
a change was his *Brand*.

IV

A MORAL SUPERMAN

I

IT sounds rather strange that *Brand*—Ibsen's gloomiest and most 'northern' work—was the first major product of his sojourn in sunny Rome, where conditions for work were ideal. What is more, this drama is imbued with the spirit of Kierkegaard's philosophy to a far greater extent than *Love's Comedy*, however reluctant Ibsen may have been to acknowledge the fact. While protesting (in a letter) against the current interpretation of his Brand as being a portrait of Kierkegaard himself, Ibsen added that he had read little and understood less of Kierkegaard's writings than people were inclined to think. But even if this be so, nothing could have precluded his contact with Kierkegaard's thoughts and ideas, many of which happened to coincide with his own. All influences apart, there was a strong *Wahlverwandtschaft* (elective affinity) between these two essentially northern geniuses; and even had Ibsen not read any of Kierkegaard's books, he might have become acquainted with their contents indirectly —by listening to their exponents at home and abroad. Whether he had ever personally spoken to Pastor Lammers (the supposed model for Brand), who from 1848 was in charge of the parish at Skien, is a matter of conjecture. During his stay in Rome, however, Ibsen had frequent talks with another Kierkegaardian, Pastor Christopher Bruun, whose integrity he greatly admired. Also the poetic and theological writings of N. F. Grundtvig, a Danish champion of religion, were much discussed by the Scandinavian élite of that period, and Ibsen was hardly a stranger to them.

Be this as it may, *Brand* is redolent of Kierkegaard's tendency to destroy the gap between faith and life. It is also imbued with his intransigent slogan, 'all or nothing', but in a somewhat one-sided manner and in Ibsen's own image as it were. For one thing, Brand's puritanic mentality is bound to strike us as being too narrow-minded, too sectarian, to be accepted by an adherent of Kierkegaard without reservations. On the other hand, one cannot

but admire (even though one may not accept his scale of values)
the tremendous impetus of his will, by virtue of which he wants
to be 'true to himself', whatever the external obstacles and difficulties. The very idea of compromise is rejected by him beforehand. The whole work breathes the spirit of these lines, taken
from Kierkegaard's fragment *Ad se ipsum*, in the section *Dia-
psalmata* of his *Either/Or*:

Let others complain that the age is wicked; my complaint is that it
is wretched, for it lacks passion. Men's thoughts are thin and flimsy
like lace, they are themselves pitiable like the lacemakers. The thoughts
of their hearts are too paltry to be sinful. For a worm it might be
regarded as sin to harbour such thoughts, but not for a being made in
the image of God. Their lusts are dull and sluggish, their passions
sleepy. They do their duty, these shopkeeping souls, but they clip
the coin a trifle, like the Jews; they think that even if the Lord keeps
ever so careful a set of books, they may still cheat Him a little. Out
upon them!

From a higher moral angle, even in a negative passion (accepted
fully and bravely) there is a greater merit than in a half-hearted
virtue, all the time wavering between good and evil.

> Be passion's slave, be pleasure's thrall,
> But be it utterly all in all!
> Be not to-day, to-morrow, one,
> Another when a year is gone;
> Be what you are with all your heart,
> And not by pieces and in part.

This singleness of will and purpose, subjecting everything to
one aim only, was as typical of Ibsen as it was of Brand. The
aim of both was unflinching devotion to that 'great task' in the
name of which they could realize themselves in this life. And
in the case of both something went wrong in the end. This is
why the figure of Brand is a remarkable piece of moral and
spiritual self-anatomy, which helped the author to penetrate into
some deeper recesses of his own personal dilemma. 'Brand is
myself in my best moments,' Ibsen said in one of his letters, and
he must have known why. Brand, like Ibsen, is also fond of
reasoning. So much so that his moralizing and theological passages often 'stick out' at the risk of encroaching upon the dramatic
side of the play. One wishes they were shorter. Yet let there be

no mistake: Brand remains a consistent personality to the end.
Being a puritan, a Pastor and a preacher by vocation, he is convincing not only when he acts, but also when he preaches. His
sermons are an expression of his character. He is, moreover, all
of a piece with the setting. The gloomy northern region, closed
to the rest of the world and in the throes of a perpetual struggle
against the evil forces of nature, is an external counterpart of his
own spiritual landscape.

II

First intended to be an epic, *Brand* was obviously inspired by
Adam Homo, a well-known romantic work of the Danish poet
F. Paludan-Müller. Soon, however, Ibsen must have found the
epic form unsatisfactory. So he put it aside and turned the
subject-matter into a drama—bulky in size yet full of unforget-
table scenes and also of that rugged beauty which is so much in
keeping with the theme as well as with the background of Brand's
exploits.

What we follow with increasing tension in this work is really
a parallelism of two conflicts brought to their dramatic climax:
one of them within Brand's consciousness, and the other in his
relations with the world, or rather with the remote little community whose spiritual needs are entrusted to his care. The
contrast between Brand the hero and the average humanity around
him is used by Ibsen as a pretext for hurling further indictments
at his countrymen. The reminiscences he had brought to Italy
from far-off Norway were none too cheerful. Even less so were
his impressions of Norway's 'cautious' behaviour during the
Prusso-Danish War. No wonder the titanic figure of Brand was
meant to be a reproach to his countrymen, and then to average
humanity in general: to all that is 'light-heart, faint-heart and
wild-heart'. Determined to realize himself fully in the name of
a great task, which he regards as being allotted to him by God,
he goes to it without swerving for a moment from the chosen path.
Hence his emphasis on the heroic aspect of the will.

> It is Will alone that matters,
> Will alone that mars and makes,
> Will that no distraction scatters,
> And that no resistance breaks.

What he wants to achieve is nothing less than a moral regeneration of all life and most particularly of the age he is compelled
to live in.

> It is our age whose pining flesh
> Craves burial at these hands of mine.

Only in fulfilling such a mission does he think he is true to
himself, and the method by which he hopes to achieve it is that
of the Kierkegaardian 'all or nothing'. Yet by applying this slogan
to a strictly moral conception of life with its uncompromising
antithesis of 'flesh' and spirit, he narrows down the compass of
his purpose, as well as of his vision. The perspective in which he
sees man's existence is thus likely to become the more distorted
the more heroically he insists on his 'all or nothing', until he finds
himself at last in a tragic collision with life as a whole. His revolt
against 'flesh' makes one think of the early Christians, of the
hermits in the Thebaid. Yet his God, far from being that of
conventional Christianity, is nearer to the stern Old Testament
Jehovah, rejuvenated by a strong injection of Viking blood. Brand
certainly does not mince words when describing—quite in the
spirit of Kierkegaard—the official Christian God as a climax of
weakness.

> You need, such feebleness to brook,
> A God who'll through his fingers look,
> Who, like yourselves, is hoary grown,
> And keeps a cap for his bald crown.

Brand's God is altogether different: a God whose voice

> —rang through the dazzled night
> When He, within the burning wood,
> By Moses upon Horeb's height
> As by a pygmy's pygmy stood.
> In Gideon's vale he stayed the sun,
>   And wonders without end has done,
> And wonders without end would do,
> Were not the age grown sick—like you.

While identifying his own will and purpose with the law of
God, Brand proceeds to attack everything that does not come up
to his own moral standard. He would not make the slightest
concession to human frailties. Love in the sense of Christian
caritas is foreign to him. His antinomic attitude towards 'flesh'

and 'spirit' as the two utterly incompatible elements is in essence a northern version of the Manichean ideal of purity, in the restoration of which he sees a calling bestowed upon him from on high. The whole drama is imbued also with the Protestant (or rather Calvinist) feeling of guilt. It is guilt devoid of any notion of Grace and overshadowed by the thought of retribution not only for one's own misdeeds, but for those of one's parents, too, and of one's parents' parents.

The very heroism of such an attitude can amount, however, to a kind of perversion from the moral end. What Brand really wants is not a broader, sunnier and happier life, but a strictly puritanic life—at the risk of turning his militant puritanism into a Procrustean bed where all that goes beyond its size is chopped off without mercy. Even normal joys and pleasures are frowned at as sinful frivolities, which ought to be sacrificed lock, stock and barrel to one's ideal of moral perfection. The slogan 'all or nothing' thus renders Brand hard and heartless, though not loveless; and this makes him the more tragic. There is much love that secretly glows in him, but he either represses it or sacrifices it to his task and his mania for moral purity. One of the most moving scenes in the drama is towards the end of the third act when Brand, compelled to make a choice between the life of his little son Alph and his own exalted duty or calling, chooses the latter and sobbingly breaks down. He is sincerely fond even of his own miserly mother; yet he refuses to see her on her deathbed, because of her unwillingness to part with the last farthing of her hoarded wealth. This is how an excess of moral zeal cripples morality itself and often turns it into its own opposite—by rendering it inhuman.

III

The antinomic character of the *leitmotif* of this drama is shown at its beginning: when Brand meets his former school-friend Einar. Einar and his fiancée Agnes are on a pleasure trip which they both regard as a prelude to a future full of joy and sunshine:

> In sunshine lies our destined way,
> And ends but with a hundred years.
> A hundred years to revel given,
> Each night the bridal lamp aflame—
> A century of glorious game.

But Brand the puritan is already there with his mournful rebuke:

> Ye will but laugh and love and play,
> A little doctrine take on trust,
> And all the bitter burden thrust
> On One who came, you have been told,
> And from your shoulders took away
> Your great transgressions manifold.
> He bore for you the cross, the lance—
> Ye therefore have full leave to dance;
> Dance then,—but where your dancing ends
> Is quite another thing, my friends.

This 'quite another thing, my friends', is what Brand cares for—to the exclusion of everything else. He puts the moral meaning of life not only above joys and pleasures, but above life itself. And since he cannot think of that meaning otherwise than in terms of will and moral duty, he demonstrates his devotion to both on the spot by braving all the elements of nature in order to bring the last comfort to a man dying on the other side of the stormy lake. Agnes, impressed by Brand's courage, joins him in his dangerous crossing and later becomes his wife.

The married life of Brand and Agnes has nothing to do with that ridiculed in *Love's Comedy*. This time we see a real union of love and marriage for the sake of a higher task here on earth. It is, of course, the task of Brand, since Agnes confines herself mainly to the rôle of devoted helper and comforter. Having first dreamt of a large field of activities where he may influence and convert thousands of human hearts, Brand takes upon himself the much sterner task of remaining in one of the bleak parishes in the north, which happens to be his native district. Agnes stands by him with courage, despite the inclemency of nature and the primitive conditions she has to put up with. Brand, however, seems to be in his proper element. His arduous exertions make him look amidst his parishioners 'like a wolf among the geese', although Agnes cannot help suspecting, now and then, that behind his moral heroism there may be a great deal of unconscious pride:

> How stern! It is thy pride of will
> That scorns the darkness and the chill.

Brand's dying mother is right in her own way when hopefully saying that the Lord Himself cannot be so cruel as her son. On the other hand, his devotion to duty impresses the simple folk accustomed to all the harshness of nature, and the number of Brand's followers grows swiftly enough to alarm the 'humane' local authorities. Meanwhile, his baby-son Alph becomes ill. The only chance of saving his life would be to accept a parish with a milder climate farther south. But Brand will not listen to the doctor's advice. To abandon his post at that juncture would be a proof of weakness, of his lack of trust in the Lord. With anguish in their hearts, Brand and Agnes stay on, hoping against hope that the Lord will spare their little Alph. The Lord refuses to spare him. But this only makes Brand more ruthless in the fulfilment of his duty. On a chilly Christmas eve, Agnes, unable to bear her bereavement, takes out her deceased baby's garments and contemplates them with motherly tenderness. Her husband sees in this, too, only a sign of weakness, and promptly orders her to give the garments away to a strayed gipsy woman and her child. Agnes obeys him without murmur, but this ultimate sacrifice breaks her heart and even her will to live. Like one who in her sorrow has 'seen Jehovah' face to face, she knows that her end is near, and the scene where she takes leave of Brand is almost unbearable in its simple pathos.

His wife and son dead, Brand is more isolated than ever, but he does not deviate one inch from his calling. With the money inherited from his mother, he builds a spacious new church which is due to be opened and consecrated amidst a large congregation of people. A brief talk with the Provost makes Brand so disgusted with the opportunism of the official church that he refuses to have the building consecrated at all. Instead of delivering the kind of sermon one usually expects on such occasions, he addresses the crowd with a fiery invitation to leave the valley and to follow him to a different Church—high up among the peaks surging freely towards God's sky. Stirred by his words, most of the crowd join him, as if he were a new Messiah, and the ascent begins. But once the promised heights have been reached, they are cold and barren. Overcome by thirst, by hunger, the weary crowd begins to murmur and even to rebel against Brand, who at the crucial moment is unable to offer them anything except a new series of sacrifices for the greater glory of moral perfection. Finally, he is driven away by his indignant followers and almost stoned to death. But here, just in time, the 'cunning vultures of the law' (the Sheriff and the Provost) appear and take good care that the crowd should go back to their huts in the valley. The Sheriff promptly concocts the yarn that huge shoals of herring have appeared in the fjord waiting to be caught, and the trick is done: everyone is in a hurry to reach the fjord as quickly as he can, while Brand—cursed and bleeding—is left among the peaks. High up in the mountains his final agony takes place, and together with it, the judgment, the 'doomsday' is held over him and his calling.

IV

It is Brand's delirium, with its visions and hallucinations, that brings his dilemma, or rather the flaws of his dilemma, to a head. All is expressed in symbols and allegories, which keep tormenting his mind. Even the mad Gerd (an illegitimate daughter the rejected penniless wooer of Brand's mother had had with a gipsy woman), familiar to Brand from former encounters, reappears now as an embodiment of parental guilt which has to be expiated. Excluded from human community, Gerd is as isolated among the mountain peaks as the self-centred Brand is on his moral heights. Both are remote from ordinary humanity, and the isolation of both verges on madness, full of haunting ghosts. Gerd actually tempts Brand with the allurements of that moral pride which (as Agnes suspected) had always been prowling at the back of his deified and self-righteous puritanic will. At the same time the phantom of the dead Agnes seeks to entice him into the spirit of mercy—regarded by him as weakness. Other delusions appear, or else are heard, arising out of the conflict in his unconscious, until he is compelled to question the value and the efficacy of his will. Who is he, anyway, to presume to be the chosen instrument of God Himself? An answer is given by the Invisible Choir, the mocking voices of which he hears during his agony:

> Worm, thou may'st not win His spirit—
> For Death's cup thou hast consumed:
> Fear his will, or do not fear it,
> Equally thy work is doomed.

In the maze of perplexities, Brand's 'pride of will' is shaken to its foundation by the sudden feeling of his own impotence. The idea that in making—under the pretext of a higher calling—his morality of repression an end in itself, he had been all the time not a saint but only a fanatic, creeps in. Does life consist of mere sacrifices, of gloom and puritanic practices upon oneself and others? Are joy, warmth, beauty, and serene kindness of so little importance that they should be excluded from life? As though overwhelmed by the futility of his ascetic past, Brand seems to heed the yearnings which, until then, had been silenced under the crust of his moral pride.

> Hence! A thousand miles away!—
> How I long to fly afar,
> Where the sunlight and the balm
> And the holy hush of calm,
> And Life's summer kingdoms are!

For the first time he feels that intransigent one-sided puritanism may be something different from, or even hostile to, the spirit of Christ, who never separated Law from mercy.

> Jesus, I have cried and pleaded
> From Thy bosom still outcast;
> Thou hast pass'd me by unheeded,
> As a well-worn word is passed.
> Of salvation's vesture, stained
> Let me clasp one fold at last.

The humility with which he utters this prayer is not in vain. Something seems to have melted in the depths of his heart. 'Radiant and with an air of renewed youth,' he catches a few beams of that light which until then must have been obstructed by the cold and rigid Law. The self-centred puritan in him seems to be giving way to the Christian.

> Through the Law an ice-track led—
> Then broke summer overhead!
> Till to-day I strove alone
> To be God's pure tablet-stone;
> From to-day my life shall stream
> Lambent glowing, as a dream.
> The ice-fetters break away.
> I can weep—and kneel—and pray.

Having shaken off the ice-fetters of the Law for its own sake, he is on the verge of religion as distinct from mere morality. But even in this new state he still remains subject to retribution—not only for his own but also for his mother's faults. The mad Gerd, whose appearance in the world had been due to the greed of Brand's mother, fires a shot at one of her own disturbing apparitions. Her shot loosens an avalanche, the rumbling of which comes nearer and nearer. Brand, filled with death-anguish, wants to have at least some assurance that his titanic will and effort had not been entirely wasted.

> God, I plunge into death's night,
> Shall they wholly miss Thy light
> Who unto man's utmost might
> Willed——?

But the answer heard through the thunder of the avalanche is itself an accusation of Brand—an accusation in five words only:

> He is God of Love.

This final truth flashes through Brand's mind when it is already too late. Retribution, inexorable as ever, takes its own.

v

The question is obviously reduced to one of the difference between a full life and a morally perfect life. That synthesis between faith and life which Brand aimed at cannot, perhaps, be achieved on a moral plane only, but in that broader religious dispensation which includes morality and at the same time transcends it. After all, the slogan 'Be true to thyself' must be raised to the transcendental religious plane, for otherwise it can easily degenerate into moral solipsism and 'pride of will'. Ignoring the fact that Christ Himself had condemned the Law devoid of mercy, Brand became a martyr of the Law and of his own self-centred puritanism. In a way he was as far from Christ as he was (for entirely different reasons) from that official church at which he hurled so many sarcasms. Blinded by his will and his sterile perfection, he could not see what Agnes saw clearly when compelled to sacrifice her last motherly solace to her husband's 'all or nothing':

Closed, all closed with bolt and bar!
Seals on every passion set!
Seal'd the grave and seal'd the sky,
Seal'd to feel and to forget!
I will out! I gasp for breath
In this lonely house of death.

A strong moral will, devoid of an adequate religious consciousness, may thus become hostile to life simply by using the latter
as a means, or a pretext, for recording the feats of one's virtue.
Did not the 'converted' Tolstoy eventually turn morality (or
what he regarded as such) against life itself? Yet what is one
to do if one lacks that deeper religious sense which alone might,
perhaps, truly integrate morality and life? It was not Ibsen's
fault that of the three elements, the ethical, the aesthetic, and the
religious (so strongly differentiated by Kierkegaard), the last one
was weak in him, as it is in thousands of moderns, the best of
whom honestly confess it—not without regret.

Such a defect does not preclude, however, a highly developed
conscience. It often happens that people devoid of the religious
sense cling all the more rigidly to the Law, as if suspecting that
but for it they would have nothing to fall back upon and would
be at the mercy of moral nihilism with its destructive 'all things
are lawful'. Yet moral perfection outside the religious plane is
usually too much aware of itself not to fall a prey to moral pride
and smugness. Such pride, whether voluntary or not, always
isolates, and isolation makes one hard. Ibsen, who was a product
of the Protestant-puritanic upbringing, was quite aware of this
tendency within himself. His analysis of Brand was therefore to
a large extent a process of self-analysis in disguise. However
sincere his quest for man's realization on earth may have been,
he stumbled here over obstacles which had to be explored more
thoroughly before he could go any further. So he approached the
dilemma from its opposite end in *Peer Gynt*.

V

THE 'GYNTISH SELF'

I

ENCOURAGED by the success of *Brand* and undoubtedly still under the impact of the creative verve with which he had written it, Ibsen finished—mostly in Ischia and at Sorrento —its satirical counterpart, *Peer Gynt*, in a few months. The two works are complementary. Their principal figures, if taken in a symbolic sense, are as interdependent as, say, Faust and Mephistopheles, or Don Quixote and Sancho Panza. Like these, they are both latent in every human being. Hence their universal appeal, despite the fact that in *Brand* the background is exclusively, and in *Peer Gynt* predominantly, Norwegian. If the first of these two works is more intense, the second is decidedly more varied in its scheme, its moods, and its fanciful artistic pattern.

In *Brand* Ibsen had to preserve the tone of a preacher, talking from a level altogether different from that of the common run of humanity. Peer Gynt, however, is on the same level as his fellow-beings and often on a lower one. He is a kind of Everyman in his more wayward, capricious, and eccentric aspects. This is why this play is in the realm of satirical comedy which only in the last act assumes a tragic turn. In *Brand* Ibsen lashed his country-men with words of fire; here ridicule and malicious laughter are his weapons. Even his amusing folkloristic and topical passages harbour more malice than their surface might suggest; and some-times even a deeper meaning than the author may have put into them at first. The trolls in the cave of Dovre, for instance, with their slogan 'Troll, to thyself be enough!' were originally a skit on those complacent nationalists who advocated utter political and economic isolationism for Norway. Yet the philosophic impact the trolls' motto acquires in the play goes far beyond the topicalities of this kind. More obscure and confusing are the grotesque allegories in the madhouse at Cairo; but Ibsen makes up for it by the powerful concreteness of such characters as Peer and his mother Aase.

Peer Gynt is supposed to depict above all the Norwegian character as seen by the author at the time he wrote the play. As it happened, the figure of Peer was based on an actual adventurer of the same name, who had lived towards the end of the eighteenth century in the Gudbrandsdal district and some of whose deeds, imaginary or real, are recorded in *Norwegian Fairy Tales* by Asbjörnson and Moe. Ibsen himself may have heard some tales about him in 1862, when he was commissioned to collect folkloristic material in the same region. It should be borne in mind, though, that here he is not in the least concerned with folklore *qua* folklore (as he often was during his Bergen period), but with his wish to express by a shorthand artistic method certain things which otherwise might have been difficult to convey.

II

Ibsen, with his antinomic habits of thought, wanted to present in the figure of Peer Gynt an antithesis of Brand, as well as a somewhat unfair symbol of the Norwegian nation in general. Yet in spite of the critical mood in which the play was written, Peer is not altogether a compendium of negative features. The material he is made of is potentially good. What he lacks, though, is that moral fibre and that inner backbone without which one's true self can never be built or realized.

This brings us once again to the Kierkegaardian principle, 'Be true to thyself', the utter distortion and caricature of which is embodied in Peer Gynt. He may be endowed with certain good qualities, such as imagination, adventurous spirit, *bonhomie*, and even occasional generosity; but on the other hand, he is so irresponsible in all the big issues that it would be futile to look in him for any singleness of purpose, let alone moral will in Brand's sense. A braggart and a voluptuary by nature, he is always prone to satisfy his vanity by wishful thinking, i.e. by all sorts of imaginary adventures which are real to him as long as he is the centre of all the happenings. He is doomed to live in lies, the mazes of which he can never quite disentangle, since the dividing line between the true and the false does not exist for him at all. In contrast to Brand's unbending straight line of moral ruthlessness, for the sake of one's self-realization, Peer prefers the much easier path of self-indulgence. The slogan, 'Troll, *to thyself be enough*', can be applied to him and his kind literally. His is the crooked way of compromise (symbolized in the figure of Böig) with himself, with life, with God and the devil. More than ready to snatch at random any pleasure that comes his way, he lets all moral laws and appeals take care of themselves. But since he wants to indulge in the line of least resistance with good conscience, he construes a whole philosophy to this effect—that peculiar philosophy of the 'Gyntish Self' which is a parody of Kierkegaard's individualism and the reverse of everything Brand stood for.

> The Gyntish Self—it is the host
> Of wishes, appetites, desires—
> The Gyntish Self, it is the sea
> Of fancies, exigencies, claims,
> All that, in short, makes my breast heave,
> And whereby I as I exist.

As the opposite pole of Brand's stern 'all or nothing', Peer Gynt is all *and* nothing. Instead of being an individualist in a deeper sense, he is an intensified egoist. Ignoring all ethical norms and values, he surrenders to the quantitative side of existence. Things that happen to him are not regulated from within, but come from without—casually, without rhyme or reason. The same applies to his numerous professions and occupations. A village ne'er-do-well at first, he becomes with the same insouciance an outlaw, a troll-woman's lover, a slave-trader, a Bible-trader, a cosmopolitan financier, a Mohammedan 'prophet', a 'scientist', anything you like—for the very reason that in reality he is nothing: 'To-day, to-morrow, one—another when a year is gone.' In his egoism (as distinct from individualism), he squanders his true self bit by bit. He does so with gusto, and never gives a single thought to the consequences that await him at the end of such a career. And when nevertheless he has to face them, he escapes from the worst owing only to something like an unexpected miracle. But here a new element—that embodied in Solveig—comes into the play as one of the ingredients of its thematic and philosophic pattern.

III

In spite of his squalid adventures with Ingrid, then with the troll's daughter (from whom he had a child), and with the three cowmaids in the mountains, Peer's capacity for true love was not

entirely dead. In fact, it flared up as soon as he met Solveig—
the woman through whose love he might have realized, under
certain conditions, his better self. Ibsen's Solveig is a new variety
of Gretchen: an apotheosis of the eternal feminine, the craving
for which is latent—according to Ibsen—in the heart of every
man. After Solveig had abandoned her family in order to join
Peer in the mountains as his sweetheart and wife, all that was
best in him awoke for a while. But no sooner had he finished the
log cabin they were to live in than the first instalment of the
retribution for his past came: in the shape of the troll's bedraggled
daughter and her monstrous little brat—Peer's illegitimate son
(a reminder of the consequences of Ibsen's own adventure with
the maidservant—perhaps a cowmaid—at Grimstad). After such
an encounter he could not face Solveig again, but fled away from
her and from the land of his shameful past. The only person he
said good-bye to (in a dramatically superb and most moving
scene) was his dying mother, to whom he was infinitely kinder
than the moralist Brand had been to his. Like Ibsen, Peer Gynt
spent most of his adult life in foreign parts, where in his own
way he 'made good' and became a wealthy if somewhat bragging
cosmopolitan. Yet far away from Solveig's influence, he relapsed
into all the pitfalls of his 'Gyntish Self'. Hence the tragi-comedy
of his exploits.

Several years after his escape from Norway, we meet him on
the African coast as a plutocrat with a thoroughly international
outlook—in matters of finance. In the style of a *nouveau riche* he
holds forth to his equally unscrupulous British, German, and
French colleagues, who soon rob him of all his treasures but are
drowned together with the ship they had stolen from him. Peer
finds consolation in a not very edifying idyll with the desert slut,
Anitra, after which he leaves for Egypt. Amidst the pyramids of
Gizeh he comes across a certain Dr. Begriffenfeld—a German
philosopher from Berlin with whose ideas he has much in common.
The learned doctor is in ecstasy over Peer's theory of the 'Gyntish
Self', since the latter happens to coincide with the tenets of his
own cult, to the temple of which—the madhouse of Cairo—he
invites Peer as an honoured guest. No sooner, however, has Peer
entered the precincts of the 'temple' than he is intuitively recognized by all its inmates as their legitimate chief, their monarch,
who ought to be crowned with the rites due to such a rank. Their

enthusiasm is spurred on by Dr. Begriffenfeld's chanted *credo* of
their own 'Gyntish selves':

> We go, full sail, as our very selves,
> Each one shuts himself in the barrel of self,
> In the self-fermentation he dives to the bottom—
> With the self-bung he seals it hermetically,
> And seasons the staves in the well of self.
> No one has tears for the other's woes;
> No one has mind for the other's ideas.
> We are our very selves, both in thought and tone,
> Ourselves to the spring-board's uttermost verge.

Surrounded by the hubbub of the lunatics, who are about to
crown him as the great egoist and 'Emperor of Himself', Peer
Gynt faints sprawling in the filth on the floor. But this does not
disturb the solemn nature of the occasion.

> Ha! see him in the mire enthroned,
> Beside himself—to crown him now!
> Long live, long live the Self-hood's Kaiser!
> *Es lebe hoch der grosse Peer!*

But if egoistic self-centredness, pushed to its limits, can end
in lunacy, it can also lead to a slow and painful awakening. Peer's
awakening, which comes late enough, is at the same time (as in
Brand's case) also a 'doomsday' over him. There is no reason
to suppose, as some critics have done, that the entire fifth act
takes place after Peer's death. What we see is merely a final
reaction in those deeper layers of his consciousness which he had
shunned as long as he could, without suspecting that sooner or
later the hour of reckoning was bound to strike. Peer, a dis-
illusioned old man but still the same egoist as ever, has come to
the end of his adventures and is in need of rest. While sailing
back to the haunts of his early youth in Norway, he passes through
a shipwreck in which he saves his life by callously letting the
ship's cook drown, knowing full well that the cook's orphaned
children at home are thereby doomed to starve. But once he sees
again the places of his youthful exploits, the truth about his life
begins to dawn on him. Pondering over his past, he now dimly
guesses that selfishness has destroyed his true self and that at the
end of his hectic life he has been left without any kernel—like
the wild onion he picks and peels on the way:

To the innermost centre is nothing but swathing—
Each smaller and smaller. Nature is witty!

Strange voices—his unthought thoughts, unsung songs, unshed
tears, unachieved deeds—pursue him like ghosts, demanding an
account which cannot be rendered. At the cross-roads he is,
moreover, stopped by the mysterious Button Moulder liable to
melt down into an amorphous mass all those humans who, in one
way or another, have failed to create and realize their true selves.
Personality in this sense is not something given, but something
that should be created by each individual. If anything in man is
likely to survive at all, it is his true self; and a person devoid of
it has no chance of survival. As Peer is one of such culprits,
the Button Moulder claims his soul as something that ought to
be destroyed like worthless rubbish for ever. Frightened by the
prospect of being snuffed out for all eternity, Peer looks for
excuses which might extenuate his guilt. He even pleads that in
essence he had never been a really great sinner, a monster, but
just something of an average bad lad—

> I am sure I deserve better treatment than this;
> I am not nearly so bad as you think—
> Indeed I've done more or less good in the world;
> At worst you may call me a sort of a bungler,
> But certainly not an exceptional sinner.

This fails, however, to placate the Button Moulder, who cuts
him short on the spot:

> Why, that is precisely the rub, my man!
> You're no sinner at all in the higher sense;
> That's why you are excused all the torture pangs,
> And, like others, land in the casting-ladle.

In short, an irresponsible nonentity cannot even be a thorough
sinner, in so far as a great sin, too, presupposes a strong personality
—even if this be only of a negative kind. Luther's rebellious
pecca fortiter (sin bravely) is, after all, ethically preferable to a
cowardly and calculating virtue. Peer has not realized himself
either in a positive or in a negative way; so he is doomed. The
problem is puzzling enough to make him ponder for a while, after
which he suddenly turns to the Button Moulder.

PEER: One question—just one.
                            What is at bottom this being oneself?

THE BUTTON MOULDER: To be oneself is: to slay oneself,
                            But on you that answer is doubly lost,
                            And therefore we'll say: to stand everywhere
                            With *Master's intention* displayed like a sign-
                                board.

PEER: But suppose a man never comes to know
                            What Master meant with him?

THE BUTTON MOULDER: He must divine it.

PEER: But how often are divinings beside the mark—
                            Then one is carried *ad undas* in middle career.

THE BUTTON MOULDER: That is certain, Peer Gynt, in default of
                                divining
                            The cloven-hoofed gentleman finds his best
                                hook.

PEER: This matter is excessively complicated.

IV

It proved to be complicated indeed, and in more respects than
one. Was not Brand firmly convinced that all his actions were
according to the 'Master's intention'—only to discover at the end
that he was wrong? Who then is morally responsible for such a
faux pas—the 'Master' or the victim? And why should the
punishment fall upon the victim? The whole problem may assume
a different aspect only in the ontological realm, where the adage,
'To be oneself is to slay oneself' (i.e. one's Gyntish self), no longer
sounds like a paradox. Peer is compelled to own that in this
deeper sense he has never been a personality, but just a bundle
of caprices, appetites, and desires, the gratification of which was
the main function of his existence.

> I no longer plead being myself,
> It might not be easy to get proven,
> That part of my case I must look at as lost.

The only thing left to him is to resign himself to the fate of
one who has trampled the earth to no purpose. Once the emptiness of his life has become clear to him, he knows that neither
regret nor repentance can be of any avail now that there is no
road back.

> I will clamber high, to the dizziest peak;
> I will look once more on the rising sun,
> Gaze till I'm tired o'er the promised land,
> Then try to get snowdrifts piled over me,
> They can write about them: Here no One lies buried . . .
> I fear I was dead long before I died.

Such is Peer Gynt's verdict on himself. Yet, like Goethe's Faust, he too is saved—though perhaps with less justification—at the last moment. Solveig, who during his years of self-indulgence kept waiting for him in the log cabin he once had built, still cherishes in her heart the image of Peer as she once had known him through her (and his) love: Peer's self at its best. It is in front of Solveig's hut that Peer, pressed by the Button Moulder for the last time to produce a self or else to perish for ever, utters the desperate cry:

> Where was I as myself, as the whole man, the true man?
> Where was I, with God's sigil upon my brow?

'In my faith, in my hope, in my love,' Solveig's answer resounds from the hut.

The Button Moulder's power over him is broken. Peer can now prove that his true self exists, after all, since Solveig has been watching over it as a mother watches over her child, and has come to its rescue at the moment of supreme peril. His gratitude is expressed in his last and rather cryptic exclamation before he dies: 'My mother! My wife!' Whereas on the physical plane Solveig is his wife, on the plane of spirit she has been his mother, without whose protection his self would have disappeared for ever.

v

In *Brand* and *Peer Gynt* Ibsen approached the problem of self-realization from its two opposite ends. In either case the issue remained inconclusive. Brand fulfilled the Law at the expense of the joys and happiness of life, and yet he failed. Peer Gynt indulged in all the joys and pleasures at the expense of the moral Law, and failed even more miserably; so miserably indeed that but for Solveig's intercession (somewhat reminiscent of a *deus*—or in this case *dea—ex machina*) nothing would have saved him. The dilemma itself was, however, much too involved and too important to be abandoned at this stage. So Ibsen took it up again in *Emperor and Galilean*. But before analysing this work, something should be said about the effect the reception of *Peer Gynt* had on its author.

Whereas *Brand* had been acknowledged all over Scandinavia as a masterpiece, the opinions with regard to *Peer Gynt* varied considerably. Many people took offence at its satirical passages. Even some of the leading critics (such as Clemens Petersen in Copenhagen) refused to see any beauty in this most original work. Petersen actually declared it to be a piece of polemical journalism which fell short of both art and reality. But Ibsen was no longer a counterpart of Earl Skule in literature. His stay abroad, as well as the success of *Brand*, had increased his self-confidence and his faith in the rightness of a work into which he had put so much of his own personal quest. His anger can be imagined. Nor did he mince words. 'My work is poetry, and if it is not, it will be poetry,' he wrote to Björnson apropos of *Peer Gynt*. 'The attitude towards poetry will have to change among us, at home, so as to conform to my work.'

He was not wrong. In a few years' time, *Peer Gynt* was generally accepted as one of the great achievements of modern literature. Later it made a triumphant tour of the stages, including the Moscow Arts Theatre. In spite of its technical and other difficulties, it still continues to be one of the favourite 'highbrow' plays in the international repertory—a distinction which it is not likely to lose.

VI

THE PARADOX OF WILL

I

ONE could hardly imagine a greater external contrast than that between *Brand* and *Peer Gynt* on the one hand, and *Emperor and Galilean* on the other. Yet whatever the differences in the subject-matter, the characters, the setting, and the period of action, Ibsen's *leitmotif* (man's self-realization on earth) dominates all three works. In *Emperor and Galilean* he makes, moreover, his last excursion into history: not the history of Norway, but that of Byzantium in the fourth century, when paganism in its agony suddenly flared up against the rising Christianity only to show its own impotence in the ensuing conflict. Ibsen chose that period not only because of the dramatic material he found in it. What attracted him was the philosophy, emanating from the very magnitude of the events depicted. 'My play deals with the struggle between two irreconcilable powers in the life of the world,' he said—'a struggle which always repeats itself. Because of this universality I call the book a world-historical drama.'

It is true that the overwhelming historical as well as philosophic material proved much too resistant even for Ibsen. But he refused to give up the task he had so much at heart. As a result, he produced a panorama of episodes and conflicts, impressive in their grandeur even if the play as a whole may justly be looked upon as a brilliant failure. Ibsen first called this work a world-drama (*Verdensdrama*), but later gave it the less ambitious title of: a 'world-historical play' (*et verdens historisk Skuespiel*) which he divided into two parts, *Julian's Apostasy* and *Emperor Julian*—each of them in five acts. The idea of writing such a work came to him as early as during his first months in Rome, that is, years before it appeared in print. One of Ibsen's Scandinavian friends, Professor Lorentz Dietrichson, who spent the summer holidays of 1864 together with him by Lake Nemi, mentions the following episode in his reminiscences:

I remember that on one occasion I was reading aloud *The Description of the Life of Julian the Apostate* by Ammianus Marcellinus. Ibsen became unusually interested in the theme. We had a lively talk about Julian, and I know that from that day on Ibsen seriously thought of working out this subject in a drama. Anyway, at the end of our talk he expressed the hope that no one would steal the theme from him.

In September of the same year, Ibsen mentioned in a letter to Björnson that he had in preparation a tragedy, *Julian the Apostate*—a 'labour which fills me with irrepressible joy'. He even hoped (so he said) to have it finished by the following summer.

If we compare these dates with that of the publication of the play in 1875, we cannot help thinking that he must have brooded over the figure of Julian a long time indeed—including the years he was working at *Brand* and *Peer Gynt*. Hence the inner link between the three works, representing as it were the three consecutive stages of the dilemma Ibsen was anxious to cope with at the time. He himself says of *Emperor and Galilean*: 'I am putting into this work a part of my own spiritual life; what I depict, I have, under other forms, myself gone through, and the historic theme I have chosen has also a much closer relation to the movement of our time than one might at first suppose.' The last sentence may refer to certain analogies between Julian's revolt against Christianity and the *Kulturkampf* in Germany, where most of the play was written. Ibsen, who had settled by then in Dresden, confessed in a letter that *Emperor and Galilean* was the first work written by him under the impact of German thought and of a more 'Teutonic' outlook. In this case it was the philosophy of Hegel, Schopenhauer, and in particular Hartmann he must have studied in the hope of clarifying the problem. On the other hand, an overdose of German thought, not quite assimilated artistically, made his 'world-historical play' rather top-heavy with philosophy.

From Ibsen's further utterances one gathers that in the course of writing this drama he did his best to preserve a more or less optimistic view of life, but without much success. 'This book will be my chief work, and it is engrossing all my thoughts and all my time,' he wrote (in July 1871) to his Danish publisher. 'That positive theory of life which the critics have demanded of

me so long, they will get in it.' Yet in September of the same
year, that is, only a few weeks later, he complained to Brandes in
a strikingly despondent mood: 'And so I ought to raise a banner,
ought I? Alas, dear friend! That would be much the same kind
of performance as Louis Napoleon's landing at Boulogne with an
eagle on his head. Later, when the hour of destiny struck, he
needed no eagle. In the course of my occupation with Julian,
I have in a way become a fatalist.' This duality of mood is
reflected throughout the play. While Ibsen the seeker and the
thinker was seriously on the look-out for some 'positive theory of
life', the sceptic in him was also at work—undermining, surrep-
titiously as it were, all his 'positive' efforts.

II

Since Ibsen himself was inclined to regard *Emperor and
Galilean* as his 'chief work', it is safe to assume that he must have
put into it more of his own mind and quest than into any of his
previous plays. But the influence German philosophic thought
had put upon him was of an ambiguous kind. If Hegel's dialectical
method promised to spur on his optimism, the teaching of
Schopenhauer and Eduard Hartmann had the opposite effect
and, anyway, played regular havoc with the dilemma he had
already tackled in *Brand* and *Peer Gynt*. For one thing, the
'Master' (whoever he may be) was now reduced—via Schopenhauer—to World-Will, the blind urge of which works through
history, through the whole of human development, according to
laws of its own. Human beings thus become mere tools and puppets of that tyrannical extra-human force, and whatever they do or
choose to do, is determined only by it: they choose what they
must and because they must. But if man's will is not his own,
then he cannot pretend to have a free destiny of his own: all is
laid down for him and imposed upon him beforehand, whether
he knows it or not. Both the individualist and the moralist in
Ibsen must have rebelled against such a possibility. And since
he was unable to accept a religious solution either, he had to
explore the whole question philosophically, while yet defending
himself against those conclusions which urged him to 'become
a fatalist'.

This time he set out to examine the dilemma of self-realization
in its world-historical significance. So his choice fell on the

5

Emperor Julian, whose apostasy from Christianity brought the antinomies of human spirit to a head not in his own person only, but in the consciousness of an entire epoch. Julian is in fact a transitional figure on a colossal world-historical scale. Born and bred a Christian, he yet cannot but resent the new Christian truth when comparing it with the glamour of the vanished or vanishing pagan beauty. The secret inner contest, from which he suffers, only makes his nostalgia for the old beauty more acute, until— after a period of vacillation between Christ and Apollo—he renounces Christ altogether and becomes a champion of paganism, in the restoration of which he sees his own great task and mission in life, indeed his destiny. But the more fanatically he opposes Christianity the more he strengthens it. Against his own will and intentions, he works all the time for the triumph of his enemy. To increase the irony of his position, he is aware of this, yet he goes on—he *has* to go on in his struggle, until there is no longer any doubt that the Christian religion must prevail because of the very persecution it has had to endure. Will and destiny are thus plainly antagonistic in Julian. His life-task is used, in a round-about way, as a mere plaything of a mysterious anonymous power even when he is sure that his actions are dictated by his own will and purpose.

Brand's 'It is Will alone that matters' was now in a blind-alley which threatened to undermine Ibsen's entire dilemma, unless he found an emergency exit. Unwilling to surrender to fatalism, he tried to modify his philosophy accordingly. What in *Brand* and *Peer Gynt* had amounted to self-realization in harmony with the 'Master's intention', now became fulfilment of one's destiny in harmony with the World-Will as working through history. To co-ordinate one's personal will and actions with the laws of this cosmic agency means to be free in necessity. The label, 'freedom in necessity', recurs again and again on the pages of *Emperor and Galilean*, but without disentangling the paradox in question. After all, whether in 'harmony' or not, everybody works for the design of the same mechanical World-Will from whose grip it is impossible to escape. Emperor Julian paved the way for Christianity precisely by trying to destroy it. His personal fate or volition was an illusion—worse, a mocking trick on the part of the World-Will. No wonder that in the course of his occupation with Julian, Ibsen had 'in a way become a fatalist'.

III

The irony of it is all the greater in view of the fact that on the surface Julian, too, like Brand, is a hero of the will. He practises the same method of repression in the name of his own ideal, but with the world as his arena. Whereas Brand wanted to suppress the 'flesh' for the sake of what he considered to be the Christian truth and spirit, Julian set out to obliterate every trace of Christianity in order to revive the pagan beauty of the 'flesh'. The contrast would be unbearably hackneyed, had not Ibsen deepened it into something more significant: into a tragedy of the human will eternally divided and torn between contradictions of the most 'ambivalent' kind.

Always 'Thou shalt'! If my soul gathered itself into one gnawing and consuming hate towards the murderer of my kin, what said the commandment: 'Love thine enemy'! If my mind, athirst for beauty, longed for scenes and rites from the bygone world of Greece, Christianity swooped down on me with its 'Seek one thing needful'. If I felt the sweet lusts of flesh towards this or that, the Prince of Renunciation terrified me with his 'Kill the body that the soul may live'. All that is human has become unlawful since the day when the seer of Galilee became the ruler of the world. Through Him, life has become death. Love and hatred, both are sins. Has he, then, transformed man's flesh and blood? Has not the earth-bound remained what he ever was? Our inmost, healthy soul rebels against it all—and yet we are to will in the very teeth of our own will. Thou shalt, shalt, shalt!

The tragedy of Julian was that he *had* to 'will in the very teeth of his own will'. He went on fighting against Christ although he must have known that after Golgotha a return to Olympus, that is, to a past stage of human consciousness, was no longer possible. In this sense the old beauty had ceased to be beautiful in the same way as the new Christian truth may cease to be true once the part played by it in the evolution of human consciousness is finished. The antitheses might only be superseded by their synthesis on a higher level, preached by Julian's mentor—the mystic Maximus, in his teaching of the 'third empire'. When Julian asked him which of the two, Christ or His opponent (the Emperor), would win, Maximus answered without hesitation:

Both shall succumb. Does not the child succumb in the youth and the youth in the man? Yet neither child nor youth perishes. . . . The

empire of the flesh is swallowed up in the empire of the spirit. But the
empire of the spirit is not final, any more than the youth is. You have
striven to hinder the youth—to hinder him from becoming a man. Oh,
fool, who have drawn your sword against that which is to be—against
the third empire, in which the twin-natured shall reign. . . . Emperor-
God—God-Emperor. Emperor in the kingdom of the spirit—and God
in that of the flesh.

One cannot help feeling that Ibsen (like Maximus) was tempted
to make Julian a champion of this 'third empire' instead of the
first, but abstained from it. Had he done so, he would indeed
have weakened or even destroyed the dramatic momentum of the
play, which demanded a clash instead of harmony and conciliation.
And the clash itself reflects the tenets of the peculiar philosophy
Ibsen was engrossed with at the time.

IV

It is not difficult to see that the idea of the 'third empire', as
put forward by Ibsen, is an ingenious blend of neo-Platonism
and of Hegel's dialectical method. Theoretically it sounded at
first plausible enough to awaken his hopes of finding 'that positive
theory of life which the critics have demanded of me so long'.
At a closer glance, however, the whole of it proved to be another
illusion. If the World-Will works like a blind ruthless machine,
we are but cogs in that machine; and whatever we will is actually
willed by it and not by us, in spite of all our philosophic theories
of freedom in necessity. 'What is worthy to live?' exclaims
Maximus, when terrified by such a conclusion. 'All is sport and
mockery. To will is to have to will.'

The ideas of will and freedom, of self-realization, of personal
calling or mission—the things which meant so much to Ibsen
the man and the dramatist, were thus threatened to the extent
of making him relegate the answer to the realm of paradoxes and
insoluble riddles rather than accept the conclusion with all its
logical and other implications. Hence the symposium at Ephesus,
where the mystic Maximus evokes several spirits in order to obtain
from them some clue to the tantalizing enigma.

'What is my mission?' [Julian addresses the first spirit.]
'To establish the Empire—by the way of freedom.'
'Speak clearly! What is the way of freedom?'

'The way of necessity.'
'And by what power?'
'By willing.'
'What shall I will?'
'What thou must.'

Hardly enlightened by the information, Julian listens to the spirit of Cain, summoned by Maximus. When asked about his own task in life, Cain answers that his mission had been to realize himself through sin.

'And what didst thou will, being thyself?'
'What I must . . .'
'And what fruit has thy sin borne?'
'The most glorious.   Life.'
'And the ground of life?'
'Death.'
'And of death?'
'Ah, that is the riddle.'

Then the spirit of Judas speaks.   Questioned as to his mission in life, Judas answers evasively:

'The twelfth wheel of the world-chariot.'
'Whither did it roll by means of thee?'
'Into the glory of glories.'
'Why didst thou help?'
'Because I willed.'
'What didst thou will?'
'What I must.'
'Who chose thee?'
'The Master.'
'Did the Master foreknow when he chose thee?'
'Ah, that is the riddle.'

Each answer only leads to a further question, the key to which seems to be beyond man's competence.   But Ibsen's chief intention was thereby to underline Julian's inner tragedy. Whereas in the first part of the play the Emperor vacillates between the 'old beauty' and the 'new truth', in the second part he stubbornly fights for his mission, while yet remaining as divided as before. One is in fact never quite sure whether he is a hero in his own name or a mere clown of the World-Will, until his rôle of tragic clown prevails. Nor is he himself sure of it either. He may force himself to think that his fight is a result of his own will and mission, but once his service is no longer required, he has to abandon the arena of history and to perish—not as a hero, but only as a tool.

'The world-will had laid an ambush for me, Maximus,' Julian exclaims, when dying of the wound inflicted by the spear of one of his own Christian soldiers. And his last words are but a confession of defeat.

'Thou hast won, Galilean!'

'Wert thou not, then, this time either the chosen one—thou victim on the altar of necessity?' laments Maximus over the dead Emperor. 'What is worthy to live? All is sport and mockery. To will is to have to will.'

V

One can imagine how Ibsen the individualist with his cult of the will must have shrunk from such a *Weltanschauung*. Even Dostoevsky, who had plunged more deeply into the same dilemma, was compelled to entrench himself behind religion rather than face all its implications. Ibsen's religious instinct was much too weak for an alternative of this kind. As a dramatist he had indeed little to gain from further excursions on those purely speculative lines. So he changed his quest, or rather the plane and the method of his quest. He turned his back on German philosophies, while confining himself to more tangible material and looking for a 'positive theory of life' elsewhere—not so much because he had promised it to his critics, but as a postulate of the militant character of his own art.

Unwilling to accept the gloomy outlook emanating from *Emperor and Galilean*, Ibsen made the sage Maximus prophesy at the end of the drama, that the third empire shall come in spite of all, and that the 'spirit of man shall re-enter its heritage' (whatever this may be). The idea of the 'third empire' actually proved much too attractive to be given up. As a tragic artist, Ibsen had to preserve at least some faith of this kind in order to counterbalance his growing notion of senselessness, chaos and evil in the world. Without such counterpoise, his art would have become merely pessimistic instead of tragic. So he was right in warding off this danger as long as he could. Yet from now on he abstained from

metaphysical speculations, and confined himself to the social and
psychological field instead. He descended from his romantic
heights to the plane of ordinary existence, and became one of the
originators of the modern realistic drama, which bears so strong
an imprint of his art and technique.

VII

IBSEN THE REALIST

I

IN *Brand, Peer Gynt* and *Emperor and Galilean*, Ibsen reached not only the maximum of mental and spiritual tension possible to him, but also that impasse beyond which he was unable or, perhaps, unwilling, to go. It was natural that he should have turned, for quite a while, to the actualities around him, as if hoping to find what room there was left in them for a 'positive theory of life'. But he was full of misgivings. In one of his poems, *A Letter in Verse* (1875), he depicted the whole of Europe as a ship sailing towards the unknown future with a corpse on board. The passengers behave as though everything were all right. Secretly, however, they feel the presence of the gruesome cargo, and the mood of uneasiness grows, as the journey goes on. This poem expresses, more or less, Ibsen's mood during that realistic period of his when he made repeated attempts to tear the shroud off the 'corpse' of contemporary life and to reveal the ugliness beneath.

The word *realism* should be used cautiously when applied to Ibsen. For he never copied reality. He was not interested in the raw material of life in the manner of a recorder of facts, but only as a creative and re-creative artist. While organising that material into a structural pattern which demanded a great deal of selection, elimination, and intensification, he never forgot that he was writing for the stage. And since he was a dramatist of ideas as well, he had to turn these into human passions and destinies within the framework of theatrical conventions. His was that kind of 'stylized' vertical realism the intensity of which often becomes symbolic without having recourse to any deliberate symbols— literary or otherwise.

Having given up his former romantic heights, Ibsen by no means abandoned the problems he was so vitally interested in. He only tackled them, from now on, on a different, i.e. social, level, as though trying to blend the creation of art with that of life. The old fighter and reformer in him was only too aware of the

72

social evils—or at least of some of them—which had to be cleared before any action of this kind could even be thought of. Ibsen the moralist, on the other hand, looked with scepticism upon the people who expected a change of man as a result of improved external conditions. For him, all change had to begin from within —as a moral process on the part of each separate individual, whose duty it was to free himself from the ballast of the old life. A change in our political and social systems could only be successful if preceded by a complete overhaul of our habitual ideas and values. 'Is it only in the domain of politics that the work of emancipation is to be permitted to go on with us?' Ibsen asked in one of his letters. 'Must not minds be emancipated first of all? Men with such slave-souls as ours cannot even make use of the liberties they already possess.'

All his personal attitudes were dictated mainly by this kind of spiritual momentum, which often made him over-simplify things that were complex by their very nature. The State, for example, that 'curse of the individual', meant to him very little precisely because he saw in its machinery only a tendency to reduce the individual to a mere political and geographic concept. 'Undermine the idea of the State,' he wrote in 1870, 'make willingness and spiritual kinship the only essentials in the case of union—and you have the beginning of a liberty that is of some value. Changing forms of government is mere toying with degrees—a little more or less—folly the whole of it.' In May 1871 he complained to Brandes: 'Is it not shameful of the commune in Paris to have gone and spoilt my excellent state-theory—or rather non-state theory? The idea is ruined for many a day; I cannot in decency even proclaim it in verse. But there is a sound kernel in it—that I see very clearly; and some day it will be put into practice, without any caricature.' And eleven years later he confessed in the same strain: 'I have not the gifts that go to make a satisfactory citizen, nor yet the gift of orthodoxy, and I keep out of what I possess no gift for. Liberty is the first and highest condition for me. At home they do not trouble very much about liberty, but about liberties—a few more, a few less, according to the standpoint of their party.'

This ethical and aristocratic anarchism was bound to restrict somewhat the field of social invectives in many of Ibsen's plays. But on the other hand, it intensified his fighting spirit, as well as his quest for those conditions in which individual men and women could realize themselves freely and fully in the very teeth of our social, political or any other taboos.

II

A foretaste of Ibsen's criticism of society was given in his *Catilina*, which was followed up by much more vigorous attacks in *Love's Comedy*, *Brand*, *Peer Gynt* and especially in the satirical comedy, *The League of Youth*. This is a purely realistic work, but it leaves one in no doubt as to the sharpness of Ibsen's claws. 'Environment has a great influence upon the forms in which the imagination creates,' wrote Ibsen in an attempt to explain the unexpected character of this play to Peter Hansen. 'Is there not something in *The League of Youth* which reminds one of sausage and beer? I do not intend by this to place the last-mentioned play on a lower level. I only mean that my point of view has changed, because here I am in a country well ordered, even to weariness.' Finished in Dresden as a kind of relaxation after *Brand* and *Peer Gynt*, it bears traces of Scribe's manner—with a dash of Gustav Freytag. It is full of comic misunderstandings, misplaced letters and farcical situations, while the pace of the action is surprisingly quick and sparkling. What gives Ibsen an advantage over Scribe, though, is his naturalness, especially his snappy realistic dialogue, taken straight from life and devoid of soliloquies and asides. His malice, expressed in terms of gaiety, only makes the play more effective: an actual fulfilment of the promise he gave (in his letter apropos of *Peer Gynt*) to Björnson that he would spare no one.

This time Ibsen chose for his target politics and politicians against the background of the provincial 'local conditions' as he had known them at Grimstad or in his native Skien. The petty political wrangles between the old and the more 'progressive' younger elements enabled the dramatist to give an authentic cross-section of the entire community, with the demagogue Stensgaard in the centre. The lawyer Stensgaard is an upstart with an unlimited lust for power, in the gratification of which he knows no scruples. Having found in the fashionable liberal clichés a possible short-cut to success, to Parliament and even further, he has become a loudspeaker of liberalism. At the same time he is most anxious to worm himself into the exclusive conservative circle of Chamberlain

Bratsberg, whose daughter Thora (with a big dowry) he regards as one of the suitable candidates for his hand. But to be on the safe side there are two other candidates in reserve, one of whom (Ragna Monsen) is discarded when her father—a vulgar financial speculator—goes bankrupt. Full of liberal words and slogans, Stensgaard is not in the least unwilling to switch over to the conservative camp, with the proviso that the coveted reward should not slip out of his hands. But the excess of his zeal is his undoing. Bratsberg literally kicks him out of his circle—back to intransigent liberalism. Through his scheming, Stensgaard forfeits even his potential consolation prize, Fru Rundholmen—the frisky and merry widow of a rich publican. Such setbacks are, however, only temporary calamities with people of his stamp. One is left in no doubt that success and the future are on his side. Which certainly does not speak well for either.

Whether or not Stensgaard is meant to be a caricature of Björnson is irrelevant at present: in a letter Ibsen himself denied it. The important thing is that in shaping him, the author knew how to intensify a highfalutin opportunist from the Norwegian provinces into the prototype of a cheap political demagogue in general. Ibsen's gift for ironic situations in particular is here displayed at its best. The same feature is conspicuous also in *The Pillars of Society*, where his realism is given a wider scope and meaning.

III

This was Ibsen's first dramatic work with a definite social accent, which we could never quite separate from his strong moral propensities.* His showing up of the 'corpse in the cargo', or of the rottenness behind the mask of respectability, looks as much dated at present as does his apotheosis of the emancipated unconventional woman, represented by Lona. All this is, however, redeemed by the well-knit structure of the play, by its dialogue, and by the manner in which Ibsen shows the Norwegian small-town *milieu* from a bigger, more significant angle. His castigating realism is miles apart from any 'Sardoudledom', or from the rhetorical fireworks of Dumas *fils*. He also makes here full *structural* use of a guilty secret overhanging the main character's

* This play, obviously a counterpart of Björnson's similar drama, *A Bankruptcy* (1875), was the first of Ibsen's works to be produced (in William Archer's adaptation) in England, at the Gaiety Theatre, on December 15th, 1880.

past: in this case the local magnate and 'pillar of society'—Consul Bernick.

It was Bernick who in his youth betrayed Lona's love by marrying her wealthy step-sister instead, thereby saving the family firm from bankruptcy. He betrayed, moreover, his best friend, Johan Tönnesen (his wife's younger brother), whom he persuaded to emigrate—together with Lona—to America and who was made, during his absence, a scapegoat for Bernick's own scandalous affair with a stray actress. The actress had mercifully died; but her illegitimate daughter, Dina, was brought up by the Bernick family in a community whose blissful smugness would have nothing to do with the world at large. Its mouthpiece, the local pedagogue Dr. Rörlund, is right in pointing to the doubt and unrest in the world beyond their little town:

The soul at war with itself; insecurity in every relation of life. See how the family is undermined!—how a brazen spirit of subversion is assailing the most vital truths! We ought to thank God that our lot is ordered as it is. A tare, alas! will now and then spring up among the wheat; but we honestly do our best to weed it out. The great point, ladies, is to keep society pure—to exclude from it all the questionable elements which an impatient age would force upon us.

The impatient age comes nevertheless right on to their threshold. Like a bolt from the blue, Lona and Johan suddenly return from America in so unconventional a manner as to shock not only their relatives, but all the respectable folk who once had known them. The town is astir with gossip and rumours, while its principal 'pillar' Consul Bernick is mortally afraid lest the secret about his own past should leak out. The private explanations he has with both Lona and Johan do not flatter his vanity. His fear of public opinion makes him sink so low indeed that, when Johan after a short stay decides to leave that stuffy atmosphere and go back to America, Bernick offers him a passage on the unseaworthy boat, the *Indian Girl,* knowing full well that the boat is doomed. As it happens, Johan and Dina (who runs away from her suitor, Dr. Rörlund) take another boat, while Bernick's adventurous little son, Olaf (a boy of twelve), stows away on the *Indian Girl* in order to join the Red Indians.

When Bernick hears of Olaf's escapade, his consternation knows no limits. What makes the situation worse is the violent storm at sea. Unless the boat is brought back in time, it is bound to go to the bottom, not only together with the crew (which is of little concern to him), but with Olaf—his only son and heir. On that very day the town is preparing a torchlight procession in honour of its most respected citizen, who has just then successfully concluded—at the expense of the town—a secret deal, promising big dividends to him and to a few other 'pillars'; but in his anguish Bernick has no thought for anything except the fate of Olaf. At the moment of the greatest tension, however, the news comes that the foreman at the wharf had, contrary to Bernick's own previous orders, retained the unseaworthy *Indian Girl* in the harbour, thus saving Olaf and those on board. The news has such an effect on Bernick as to produce in him a violent moral crisis. When the entire town, with torches and music, comes to pay homage to its paragon of public and private virtues, he voluntarily confesses all his past transgressions, including his unscrupulous recent deal. He does this in a courageous, manly style—without wailing, without self-pity or the self-humiliation, typical of Russian sinners. Bernick thus conquers his better self. Not independently, of course, but with the help of Lona who, for some reason, finds it necessary to proclaim the old platitude that Truth and Freedom are the only reliable pillars of society. A 'positive theory of life' thus triumphs after all. But not for long. Ibsen himself must have felt that something more provocative was needed in order to invest a social drama with the rôle he wanted to give it. With this in view, he wrote *A Doll's House* and *Ghosts*—the two plays which soon made his name both famous and notorious all over Europe.

IV

The principal reason for the uproar raised by them was again Ibsen's attack on marriage; not on marriage in general as in *Love's Comedy*, but on that prevalent in the modern world. Here, too, as in *The Pillars of Society* (but more subtly), the guilt is transferred to the past, and the logic of its consequences leads in both cases to a most dramatic dénouement. In *A Doll's House*, for instance, Nora's husband, a lawyer by profession, is a model family man as far as appearances go: honest, punctilious, hard-working, fond of his wife and children—in short a walking encyclopaedia of bourgeois virtues. Unaware of his own smug egoism underneath it all, he basks with relish in the halo of his respectability: not as a

conscious hypocrite like Bernick, but as an unconscious one—
which makes it worse. Still, it would be impossible to imagine a
cosier bourgeois idyll than the one presented by his family at the
beginning of the play. But since his spontaneous, childlike wife
Nora exists for him only as a doll or a pet, whose purpose in life
should be to gratify his smugness, dramatic justice demands that
the shock destroying all this should come from her. And come
it does.

Every theatre-goer remembers that Nora, ignorant of law, forged
her dying father's signature in order to borrow from the shady
money-lender, Krogstad, the means with which to take her ailing
husband to Italy and thus restore him to health. On her return to
the capital, Nora is blackmailed because of that signature at a time
when her husband has been appointed manager of an important
bank. She is made to see, before long, that there is a difference
between the dictate of one's conscience and that of public law.
Although her deed was the only way of saving her husband's life,
Krogstad makes it clear to her that such impulses mean nothing in
the eyes of the law. Baffled by it all and feeling vaguely guilty,
Nora is in mortal terror lest her 'crime', due to her love, should be
disclosed. Not that she doubts her husband's magnanimity and
understanding. For the very reason that she is so sure of him, she
prefers to contemplate suicide rather than to prejudice, by a
possible legal action, his career. The decision to take her own life
fills her with the ecstasy of despair. Helmer is, however, far from
magnanimous on learning about Nora's secret. The mere idea that
his wife might be publicly involved in a criminal case of forgery and
thus jeopardize his own future or, in any case, leave a blot on his
name, makes him behave in such a mean and cowardly way that her
eyes are suddenly opened. With astonishment she sees her husband's real character, and all the masquerade of her married life
appears to her in its true light. In a well-known scene she leaves
him. But her last words contain a vague promise that she might
return if the 'miracle of miracles' should happen; that is, if both of
them first became mature enough to transform their cohabitation
into a true marriage.

V

The morality of the period was shocked by even such a com-
paratively mild catastrophe of married life as Nora's flight. The

German theatre-goers in Berlin, Hamburg and Vienna actually prevailed upon Ibsen to alter, for the benefit of their tender moral feelings, such a dénouement. In this version Nora, when about to depart, throws a last glance at her sleeping children and with the remark, 'Oh, I sin before myself, but am unable to leave them,' remains. Fortunately, Ibsen discarded this idyllic finale in all the printed editions: by making Nora change her mind, he would have taken the sting out of the play.

We need not dwell on the feminist propaganda connected with *A Doll's House*, or on the attempts to turn Nora Helmer into a professional blue-stocking. All this is now a matter of the past. But it is well to remember that, according to his own assertion, Ibsen was here concerned not with feminism, but with 'humanity in general'. To Helmer's remark that she is first of all a wife and a mother, Nora answers that her first duty is to realize herself as a human being. Like young Selma Bratsberg at the end of *The League of Youth*, she resents the fact that she has never been given a chance of this kind by her husband.

In so far as Ibsen's own private attitude was concerned, he, of course, followed with interest all the movements which he considered progressive and a corrective to the established order. It was in this sense that he also became acquainted with the feminist movement. He was familiar with Stuart Mill's *Subjection of Women* (translated into Danish by Georg Brandes) and knew personally the authoress Camilla Collett—a champion of feminism in Norway. Yet as he himself pointed out, feminist propaganda as such was the last thing he ever had in mind. What propaganda value there is in this play at all, concerns not feminism but those ethical and spiritual factors without which marriage remains a mere 'living together'. It is Nora's sudden awakening to such a truth that makes her go away. This is why the discarding of her masquerading costume in the last scene has a symbolic meaning, made clear even to her husband. She does it with a moral lecture—it is true; but as a finale of this kind is motivated both artistically and psychologically, the play remains a masterpiece in spite of 'morals'.

Let us add that Nora Helmer is the highwater mark of Ibsen's characterization by means of contradictory small touches, welded into a complete and organic whole. A child and a heroic woman in one; irresponsible and unconsciously fibbing in small things, she yet rises to the occasion in important matters. She displays all her art of innate coquetry when hoping to induce the family friend Dr. Rank to help her out of her difficulty, but shrinks back as soon as she hears his clumsy declaration of love. Wasteful through generosity and spontaneous warmth, she increases her charms by her very defects. In this respect she represents the greatest possible contrast to her husband, whose virtues only emphasize his innate bourgeois meanness. Altogether she is a triumph of Ibsen's art.

VIII

'MANKIND HAS FAILED'

I

AN adroitly interpolated motif in *A Doll's House* concerns Helmer's friend, Dr. Rank, whose incurable disease—a retribution for his father's gay life—illustrates Ibsen's two converging ideas of fate. Belonging to an age in which the importance of the law of heredity was paramount, Ibsen worked out in *Ghosts* the moral and the biological conceptions of fate as forcefully as he could. Mrs. Alving's vain fight against the madness with which her talented artist-son Oswald has to pay for his father's debaucheries, lends the proper mood to the whole play which, technically, well-nigh preserves the three unities demanded by Aristotle from a tragedy.

'The fault is that all mankind has failed,' Ibsen wrote in the notes to this work, and he meant it. *Ghosts* is a much more daring challenge to society than *A Doll's House*. It is known that Ibsen wrote it as an answer to the objections raised by Nora's flight from her husband and children. Tied to a worse husband than Helmer, Mrs. Alving, instead of leaving him, had decided to stay, and to cover up the 'corpse' of her married life with respectable trappings. She is, of course, older, mentally more mature and—with all her sensitiveness—a stronger character than Nora Helmer. But she had incurred her first guilt in the past by marrying a man she did not love, instead of Pastor Manders, to whom at the time she was attached. Her second guilt was that she obeyed the same Pastor when he ordered her to return to the horrors of her family life rather than compromise the ideal of 'Christian' marriage by running away from it. She succeeded in saving at least appearances so well that her husband's name commanded respect in the whole district. The behind-the-scenes of her domestic life were, however, entirely different from the glittering façade. What that hell was like in reality is revealed by Mrs. Alving to Pastor Manders years after her husband's death.

To keep him at home in the evenings, and at night, I had to make myself his boon companion in his secret orgies up in his room. There I have had to sit alone with him, to clink glasses and drink with him, and to listen to his ribald, silly talk. I have had to fight with him to get him dragged to bed,—I had to bear it for my little boy's sake. But when the last insult was added: when my own servant-maid—; then I said to myself: 'This shall come to an end.' And so I took the reins into my own hand—the whole control—over him and everything else. It was then that I sent Oswald away from home. He was nearly seven years old, and was beginning to observe and ask questions, as children do. That I could not bear. It seemed to me the child must be poisoned by the merely breathing the air of that polluted home. . . . No one knows what that cost me.

II

Mrs. Alving does not lay the blame entirely on her husband. His temperament, his innate love of life, sought for adequate outlets in an atmosphere of shams and repressions which, instead of joys, offered only dissipations. And even these had to take on the shape of clandestine debaucheries. The pregnant maidservant was soon palmed off (for a considerable sum of money) on the joiner Engstrand—the principal villain and hypocrite in the gallery of Ibsen's characters. Everything was duly hushed up. Appearances were saved, while Mrs. Alving's capable management increased the family fortune. Later, for reasons of her own, she even built an orphanage in her husband's memory. It is with the final preparations for the opening of the Alving Orphanage that the play begins.

The opening itself is timed so as to coincide with Oswald's return from Paris. Oswald has already been back for some days. Yet he feels out of place and rather despondent in an atmosphere where work is looked upon as a punishment for sins, and man's life as 'something miserable, something it would be best to have done with, the sooner the better'. For he, too, is full of an innate joy of life, and this has found—so far—an outlet in his artistic calling, pursued by him abroad, far away from the gloomy North.

'Mother, have you noticed that everything I have painted has turned upon the joy of life?—always, always upon the joy of life?—light and sunshine and glorious air—and faces radiant with happiness. This is why I am afraid of remaining at home with you. . . . I am afraid lest all my instincts should be warped into ugliness.'

He, too, like so many of Ibsen's heroes, wants to combine his vocation with joy and happiness. But he does not think that his

homeland, or at any rate his rainy native district, is the proper place
for this. Besides, he feels frustrated by a mysterious disease from
which he has been suffering for a long while and which now
threatens him with insanity. He is completely in the dark as to its
origin. His own life has been clean and decent throughout. Also
the notions he has of his late father's character are such as to make
it impossible for him to imagine anything in the nature of a heredi-
tary taint. His continuous and rather puzzled brooding makes
things worse for him, but nothing can be done. Mrs. Alving, however, is only too well aware what those symptoms mean and where
they come from. Terrified by what may be in store for her only
son, she is ready to do anything in order to help him. She would
not even shrink from condoning Oswald's love for her pretty but
hard-boiled chambermaid Regina—Engstrand's 'daughter', but
actually the illegitimate half-sister of Oswald, who knows nothing
about it. There is a moment when Mrs. Alving is about to ease her
son's mind (if this be still possible) by telling him the truth about
his father's past. But her adviser, Pastor Manders, who is in
charge of all the operations connected with the orphanage, will
not hear of such an immoral intention.

'Is there no voice in your mother's heart that forbids you to destroy
your son's ideals?'
'But what about the truth?'
'But what about Ideals?'
'Oh! Ideals! Ideals! If only I weren't such a coward!'

The question is whether by being less cowardly she could have
averted Oswald's doom, since the unavoidable fate had to prevail. It even took a short cut by hastening Oswald's catastrophe
during the symbolic burning down of the orphanage—secretly set
on fire by the 'pious' carpenter Engstrand. Oswald, who all
through the night did his uttermost to save what still could be
saved of his father's memorial, is so fatigued that he collapses
towards the morning and loses his reason. The play ends with his
idiotic crying for the sun, while Mrs. Alving, crushed by despair,
stands over him—unable to decide whether it would not be better
and more humane to poison her only child rather than let him drag
on the existence of an incurable imbecile.
Ibsen would not have been himself had he not discharged, in this
gloomy piece, some of his caustic *Galgenhumor*—not as a relief,

but as a further thickening of the gloom. One cannot laugh—one only grins at the fact that the money which had been put aside for the maintenance of the Alving Orphanage is eventually allotted (by the unsuspecting Pastor Manders) to Engstrand, who intends to use it as capital investment for a brothel in disguise, with his 'daughter' Regina as one of its main attractions.

III

The impression of *Ghosts*, with its overhanging atmosphere of fate, can be tremendous. Even those who are inclined to accuse Ibsen of sensationalism cannot but admit that here a very risky theme has been handled with the greatest artistic tact. The more so because, instead of action, the play consists of a series of conversations full of that dynamic reserve which was one of Ibsen's secrets. Misgivings crop up only when one begins to analyse one's own feeling of depression at the end of it. A tragedy, however catastrophic, makes one affirm life in spite of all. Here, on the contrary, we cannot get rid of the notion that mankind has actually failed beyond repair. Mrs. Alving may be one of Ibsen's tragic heroines, yet the play as a whole remains more pessimistic than tragic. Ibsen's favourite theme of guilt-retribution (even upon children) here makes one depressed and puzzled precisely because it blends—in such a powerful realistic-symbolic manner—the moral and the biological types of retribution, without really deepening or else ennobling our perception of life.

For if there is no possibility of an ultimate higher sense in human existence; if man's life and fate can be reduced to a mere biological category with its inexorable laws of nature (heredity being one of them), then one is landed again in a hopeless determinism where 'all is sport and mockery'; where everything happens because it must. What is the use, then, of striving, of resisting? Both guilt and retribution become something imposed and mechanical, which is senseless; and the individual *qua* individual has nothing to do with either. He is only a tool; a passive victim of the same determinism. Moreover, in the case of Oswald and his father one cannot help thinking that a mechanical remedy (perhaps in the nature of salvarsan) administered in time and in sufficient quantity would probably have undone, in the same mechanical manner, the entire 'retribution'. While watching Ibsen's *Ghosts*, we may feel plenty of 'terror and pity', but since the vital *catharsis* does not take place, its pessimism remains this side of tragedy, like that of Hardy's *Jude the Obscure*, or of *The Golovlyov Family* by Saltykov-Shchedrin.

But Ibsen himself refused to submit to the blind-alley he had to face. The reformer and the striving moralist in him could not as yet contemplate a final surrender to pessimism—least of all in view of the ensuing attacks which stirred up all his warlike temper. For the world saw in *Ghosts* only a sordid blasphemy of family life. Abuse of the foulest kind kept pouring upon its author. Such a reference to his play as an 'open drain' was relatively mild. An impressive bouquet of similar epithets, gleaned from the English press of the period, can be found in Bernard Shaw's *Quintessence of Ibsenism*. It is only fair to say that in Scandinavia, where abuse was particularly virulent, *Ghosts* was defended by Brandes and Björnson. As though encouraged by them, Ibsen wrote to his publisher Hegel (March 1882): 'As regards *Ghosts*, I feel certain that the minds of the good people at home will soon be opened to its real meaning. All the infirm, decrepit creatures who have fallen upon the work, thinking to crush it, will themselves be crushed by the verdict of the history of literature.' But even without waiting for such a verdict, he answered his detractors in the shape of a new play, *An Enemy of the People*.

IV

In June 1882 Ibsen confided in a letter to the Norwegian author Jonas Lie that he was not yet sure whether to call this work a comedy or a drama, since 'it partakes of the nature of either, or lies half-way between'. The final result was a comedy, but of the most polemical and hilariously malicious kind he ever wrote. Its hero, Dr. Stockmann, obviously voices Ibsen's thoughts. The doctor's lecture in the fourth act in particular is Ibsen's own challenge to the entire 'compact majority' with its consensus of opinion. In spite of this, the pugnacious doctor stands on his own feet. One cannot but see in him a quixotically honest self-made man who is on the threshold of material success after having known both poverty and humiliation. This is why his self-righteousness is coupled with an almost childish delight in the modest luxuries he can at last afford.

We are introduced to him after he has been appointed physician to a little spa which derives considerable wealth from its curative waters. But the doctor makes the discovery that those waters are infected with some pestilential germs. He at once undertakes the measures by which he hopes to make the truth known and to remove the danger as quickly as possible. He is even sure of a reward for so important a piece of news, but his optimism receives one shock after the other. The speculators or the financial 'pillars of society', whose investments depend on the good name of the spa, are the first to demand that the truth about the germs should be hushed up without delay. Then the 'press', with its tricks, steps in as a supporter of those in power. Finally, the doctor has to face the onslaught of the entire 'compact majority', worked by propaganda into that frenzy which cannot but stifle the voice of reason. The doctor loses his post. He is booed and demonstrated against, while the members of his family are avoided like lepers by all and sundry. Nevertheless, he refuses to give in. After his spiteful lecture in the fourth act (which is the ideological as well as dramatic climax of the play), he finds sufficient strength in being able to stand alone. But he is not entirely alone. His wife and children give him moral support by rallying to him when the crisis is at its worst. So he decides to remain in the town in order to fight the pestilential foundations of its wealth to the bitter end.

It is hardly necessary to point out that Ibsen's individualism here reaches its climax. *An Enemy of the People* entirely accords with the mood illustrated by Ibsen's letter to Brandes on January 3rd, 1882:

It will never, in any case, be possible for me to join a party which has the majority on its side. Björnson says: 'The majority is always right.' And as a practical politician he is bound, I suppose, to say so. I, on the contrary, must of necessity say: 'The minority is always right.' Naturally I am not thinking of that minority of stagnationists who are left behind by the great middle party which with us is called Liberal; but I mean that minority which leads the van, and pushes on to the points which the majority has not yet reached. I mean: That man is right who has allied himself most closely with the future.

V

So much for the similarity or even identity of Ibsen's ideas with those of Dr. Stockmann. It is all the more to Ibsen's credit that his Stockmann is detached from him artistically as an independent character and remains convincing even as a preacher, since preach-ing—as in the case of Brand—is part and parcel of his nature. For in addition to being an honest provincial doctor, he is also a bourgeois descendant of Brand, though rather inclined to be carried away by his own eloquence even when the ideas enunciated by him are of a pedestrian kind. From his spirited tirades one learns that 'in a house which isn't aired—my wife, Katrine, even maintains that floors ought to be scrubbed too, but we can't discuss that now—well—in such a house, I say, within two or three years, people lose their power of acting morally. Lack of oxygen enervates the conscience.'

But this is how a provincial doctor, believing in science, would probably argue. Regarding himself as a champion of truth and honesty in all walks of life, he is worked up to such a pitch as to proclaim that all those who live upon lies should be 'exterminated like vermin'. Yet when it comes to defining the opposite of lies, all he has to say is that a 'normally constituted truth lives, as a rule, seventeen or eighteen years; at the outside twenty, seldom longer'. After which it presumably becomes a lie, a 'ghost'. But are truths of this kind really worth fighting for with such stubbornness as his? Nor is one sure where exactly the line between truth and lies could be drawn. What is more, in their preference of lies to truths, the 'compact majority' may be following an instinct which is, per-haps, of vital importance for all those who are too weak to face the truth about themselves or about life, and the majority are weaklings of precisely this kind. Destroy their convenient lies and illusions, and their lives, too, will be ruined.

The problem of truth and falsehood thus cropped up again—this time in its biological significance and function. If human beings need lies just as a cripple is in need of crutches, then the whole dilemma should, perhaps, be approached from a new angle. Supposing a weakling were deprived of crutches and all of a sudden shown the falsehood on which his life rested—would the game be worth the candle? What exactly would be the result? Questions of this kind point to the transition from *An Enemy of the People* to *The Wild Duck*, and this transition was much more logical than may at first appear. For once it was Ibsen the ironical sceptic who took the upper hand over Ibsen the moralist and fighter.

IX

THE TURNING-POINT

I

THE relation between *The Wild Duck* and *An Enemy of the People* is not unlike that between *Peer Gynt* and *Brand*. If Peer is a deliberate parody of Brand, the spirit prevailing in *The Wild Duck* can be regarded as a parody of practically everything Dr. Stockmann stands for. But whereas the undercurrent of *Peer Gynt* is still one of ardent faith, *The Wild Duck* must have been written in a mood of utter disappointment with humanity, especially with that 'average' portion of it the tragedy of which is that it cannot even be tragic. Whatever Dr. Stockmann may have advocated in Ibsen's previous play, the picture of life presented in this one is based on the idea that truth would positively be harmful to most people if they had to face it in all its nakedness. Stockmann's dictum that 'all who live on lies should be exterminated like vermin', now gives way to the opposite view, even to a deliberate apology for lies, falsehoods and illusions as something without which life would often become unbearable. As one of the characters—also a doctor—in the play puts it: 'Rob the average man of his life-illusion, and you rob him of his happiness at one stroke.'

In spite of the hidden chuckle which is often felt between the lines of *The Wild Duck*, this play is among the bitterest things Ibsen ever wrote. His principal urge, that of self-realization, is tested here on precisely such an 'average man', Hialmar Ekdal, who would not and could not part with his life-illusions and self-deceptions even if he had to. He may act before himself and before others in the name of some higher 'claims' which he does not even understand; yet after each declamatory feat of this kind he only sinks deeper into the morass of his habitual escapist attitudes, which he needs no less than he needs his daily bread.

Hialmar Ekdal's character consists in the absence of it. Having been spoilt and flattered in his youth, he underwent—like Ibsen— a reversal of fortune after his father's bankruptcy. While the 'shipwrecked old man with silver hair' (as he rhetorically calls him) sat in prison, Hialmar himself gave up his university studies and,

88

having married the former maidservant Gina, started his career as a suburban photographer. That meant a descent socially, but Hialmar was one of those weaklings who instinctively make themselves at home in whatever position is allotted to them, and always find solace in compensatory self-deceptions which become an essential part of their lives.

His profession of photographer was not exactly lucrative, but this did not debar him from a smug though modest comfort. He lived in harmony with his hard-working Gina, his slightly demented father, and the affectionate fourteen-year-old Hedvig, who adored him as only a child of that age can adore. As Gina and even little Hedvig were always glad to relieve him of photographic drudgery, he was able to abandon himself to his declamatory rhetorics and to the day-dreams about a prospective invention of his which would restore to honour the family name—so sadly ruined by his parent. In fact, he was as contented as a man of his calibre could be; and would have remained so, had not his friend Gregers Werle started interfering with his and Gina's existence.

II

Hialmar and Gregers meet after an interval of fifteen years, during which many things have happened. Greger's father is a rich industrialist, but he owes his wealth to a shabby transaction, the victim of which was old Ekdal—Hialmar's 'shipwrecked old man'. An officer and a mighty hunter in those days, Ekdal became a human derelict after the trial, and all he is now fit for is a thoroughly sheltered existence in his son's flat, where an attic, filled with a few withered Christmas trees, domesticated rabbits, hens and pigeons, has been set aside as his special 'hunting preserve'. In the same attic lives Hedvig's pet—the crippled wild duck. The bird had been winged by old Werle with grape-shot and fluttered down into the marsh. But it was rescued and later given to little Hedvig, who tamed it and became most attached to it: partly because there was no one else to take care of the lonely crippled thing.

Ekdal's former partner Werle lives on a big scale and in luxury, but the two households are strangely interwoven. After old Ekdal's disgrace, it was Werle who enabled Hialmar to learn photography and to open a professional studio. It was Werle again who, for various reasons, had been responsible for Hialmar's marriage

to the former maidservant Gina. Estranged from his nagging
and neurotic wife (Gregers's mother) Werle ran after other
women, Gina included. But when Gina became pregnant, he
quickly palmed her off on Hialmar Ekdal who had no idea of what
was behind it. The married couple settled down. Hialmar regarded
himself as the happy father of little Hedvig, and in his case ignor-
ance was certainly bliss. Nothing disturbed his suburban existence, so competently watched over by his practical if somewhat
henlike Gina who, during the fifteen years of her married life,
became sincerely attached to her husband. All this was shaken,
though, by Gregers's sudden reappearance.

Gregers Werle, with his sentimental one-track mind, is an
are-you-saved crank, all out for 'truth and integrity'. Suffering
from a strong mother-fixation, he cannot but loathe his father
(whose past he knows) to the extent of relishing any action likely
to compromise that domineering and profligate old gentleman.
Gregers is, moreover, depressed by fits of gnawing conscience,
because years before—during Ekdal's trial—he had allowed himself to be browbeaten by his parent into silence about the truth
behind that frame-up. As he is devoid of both discernment and
sense of humour, he finds it all the easier to experiment with his
'claims of the ideal' on such a harmless guinea-pig as Hialmar
Ekdal.

Having learned that Hialmar does not know or even suspect
anything about Gina's past, Gregers decides there and then that his
friend's marriage should be based not on lies and falsehood, but on
such truthfulness as would be likely to bring about an inner
transformation in both husband and wife, and thus turn their union
into a 'true marriage'. So, with the best intention in the world, he
tells Hialmar all about Gina's former connection with Werle.

But there are no signs of an inner change. Shallow though
he be, Hialmar realizes that Gregers expects of him something
lofty and highfalutin. Perfectly willing to live up to his expec-
tations (which he does not understand at all) he, therefore, acts,
repeating like a parrot his friend's idealistic slogans. But at
the same time he puts on the rôle of a profoundly injured husband,
and makes himself increasingly ridiculous, mean and vulgar,
without being in the least aware of it.

The matter-of-fact Gina, who knows what would have happened
to Hialmar and to his business had he married a less practical

woman, is rather nonplussed by all this rumpus about her old story with Werle which she herself has well-nigh forgotten. Nor does she quite follow Gregers's imbecile 'claims of what-do-you-call-it'. She becomes seriously alarmed, though, when the inquisitive prying into her past threatens to give away Hedvig's real parentage. But here the benevolently cynical Dr. Relling intervenes, enriching and also complicating the pattern of the play.

<h3 style="text-align:center">III</h3>

What makes Dr. Relling step in is his solicitude for little Hedvig. He knows who and what Hialmar is. And as for Gregers's 'claims of the ideal', he despises them as much as he does Gregers himself. Having taken a full measure of human weaknesses, he is a deliberate champion of life-lies as the only means of making existence bearable and indeed possible to the bulk of mankind. In order to live, people need at least a minimum of happiness and comfort. And since truth is conducive to neither, it would be as cruel to take away their illusions as to deprive a cripple of his much-needed crutches. It was for this reason that he promoted such a windbag as Hialmar to the status of a budding inventor. In the same breath he proclaimed the eternally drunken ex-divine Molvik a 'daemonic' character.

'That is the blister I have had to put round his neck.'
'Isn't he really daemonic then?'
'What the devil do you mean by daemonic? It is only a piece of gibberish I've invented to keep a spark of life in him. But for that the poor harmless creature would have succumbed to despair and self-contempt many a long year ago.'

The mere sight of the 'puritanic fever' with which Gregers has set about a hoped-for transformation of Hialmar and Gina makes Dr. Relling chuckle. Quite another matter is, however, little Hedvig—now on the threshold of girlhood, and therefore all the more susceptible to what is going on around her. With her attachment to Hialmar, she is not only puzzled by the discord between her parents, but feels profoundly, hysterically, unhappy. Hence the doctor's ominous warning to both of them:

'You must be good enough to keep Hedvig outside all this. You two are grown-up people; you are free, in God's name, to make what mess and muddle you please of your life. But you must deal cautiously with Hedvig, I tell you; else you may do her a great injury. . . . Or she may do herself an injury—and perhaps others too.'

His words are not heeded. Hialmar would probably have quietened down, had Gina played the part of a repentant wife—'writhing with penitence and remorse'—in the style of his own melodramatic taste. But nothing of the sort happens. Things take a sudden turn for the worse, when the simultaneous threat of blindness to Werle and to Hedvig (heredity again!) arouses a more sinister kind of suspicions in Hialmar. Werle's generous birthday gift to Hedvig seems to confirm them. Hialmar, who is really devoted to Hedvig, becomes cruel in his behaviour, and irresponsibly calls Hedvig (who is in the room) an 'interloper'. After which he goes on an all-night spree with Relling and the 'daemonic' Molvik.

Hedvig is frantic with despair. Gina, on the other hand, keeps her own practical head as cool as she can and hopes for the best. The catastrophe might have been averted but for Gregers's further meddling—this time with Hedvig. He comes upon the idea that a sacrifice on Hedvig's part might restore Hialmar's affection for her and perhaps bring about more quickly the miracle of a 'true marriage' between her parents. But little Hedvig does not grasp it.

'Suppose you were to sacrifice the wild duck, of your own free will, for his sake?'
'The wild duck?'
'Suppose you were to sacrifice, for his sake, the dearest treasure you have in the world?'
'Do you think that would do any good?'
'Try it, Hedvig.'

She promises to do so. Next morning, when the frowsy and still half-tipsy Hialmar comes back, Hedvig secretly takes old Ekdal's pistol and goes to the attic in order to sacrifice the wild duck. But while she is in the attic, Hialmar suddenly abandons himself to loud outpourings of self-pity, while holding forth to Gregers. Resentful of Werle's gift to Hedvig, he now complains that Hedvig most probably has never loved him and would, perhaps, be glad even to desert him, if tempted by Werle's riches. Hedvig, who cannot help overhearing his words, feels so outraged in her sensitive *[handwritten annotations at top of page: "Or - She cannot bear to kill the duck, must shoot himself instead. More symbolic - Being forced to shatter the illusion results in one's own death (physical or spiritual)"]*

little heart that she does not shoot the wild duck—she shoots herself instead.

Hialmar and Gina are crushed by her death. Their grief makes them forget their quarrel. But Gregers (sorrowing though he be) feels almost elated by the fact that his 'claims of the ideal' have triumphed after all—even at such a price.

'Hedvig has not died in vain. Did you not see how sorrow set free what is noble in him?'

'Most people are ennobled by the actual presence of death,' [retorts Dr. Relling, who knows better.] 'But how long do you suppose this nobility will last? . . . Before a year is over, little Hedvig will be nothing to him but a pretty theme for declamation. Then you will hear him spout about the "child too early torn from her father's heart"; then you'll see him steep himself in a syrup of sentiment and self-deception and self-pity. Just you see.'

'If you're right and I'm wrong, then life is not worth living.'

'Oh, life would be quite tolerable, after all, if only we could be rid of the confounded duns that keep pestering us, in our poverty, with the claims of the ideal.'

Such is the doctor's remark, which might serve as a Post Scriptum to the entire drama.

IV

Technically, *The Wild Duck* is one of Ibsen's best-constructed plays. In no other work of his are all the ingredients, down to the smallest details, more closely and as it were organically interwoven than they are here. Hialmar is a wonderful character-study, rendered by means of ordinary trifles and small touches. So is Gina. And so is little Hedvig—an affectionate child to her finger-tips, yet treated without a tinge of sentimentality. This time Ibsen surpasses himself also in his skill at retrospective unravelling of the culprit's past: a process which serves as the structural backbone or axis for the entire play. The crippled and sheltered wild duck, on the other hand, has a symbolic reference to quite a few of the *dramatis personae*, beginning with Hialmar and his 'shipwrecked old man with silver hair', since their lives are equally sheltered and unreal. Devoid of any substance, Hialmar, for instance, cannot but pretend, that is act, whether he wants to or not. In Ibsen's draft for *The Wild Duck* Hialmar himself confesses to

Gregers that he has been acting all the time in order to live up to his friend's 'claims', without really meaning anything by all the fuss and tumult raised in the house over Gina's past.

GREGERS: You did not mean anything by it?

HIALMAR: No, it was mostly on your account, Gregers. You came here and made such unreasonably heavy claims on me—I want everything to be pleasant and easy and comfortable.

GINA: Ekdal is not made to be unhappy.

GREGERS: I'm beginning almost to believe that.

HIALMAR: Yes, and so I am going to stay here with Gina and Hedvig, just as before.

GINA: That's right.

GREGERS: But, my dear fellow, that's exactly what I've been striving for.

HIALMAR: Yes, but you wanted it to be brought about by a lot of hocus-pocus, that I don't understand at all.

Another piece of irony: it is not Hialmar and Gina, but Gregers's hated father and his housekeeper Mrs. Sörby who eventually realize what might be called a true marriage, based on the mutual frankness of two people each of whom has a past to account for. The machine of moral retribution is thus stopped for a while— unless Werle's approaching blindness is a penalty for the sins of his youth. Anyway, the point is not made clear. Clear beyond any doubt, however, is the fact that most of Ibsen's principal themes and slogans (self-realization, great life-tasks, inner integrity, claims of the ideal, love and marriage) have met in this play chiefly in order to be used in inverted commas or even to be turned into parodies of themselves. Gregers, with his mission in life ('I found it yesterday'), is not only a deliberate caricature of Brand and Stockmann, but also of Ibsen the romantic, who now seems tacitly to agree with Dr. Relling's dictum that there is an excellent native word for ideals—namely, life-lies; the two being 'just about as closely related as typhus and putrid fever'.

V

In the letter he sent, together with the MS., to his publishers, Ibsen stated that 'in some ways this play occupies among my dramatic works a position by itself; in its method it differs in several respects from my previous plays. But I shall say no more on this subject at present.' What exactly he meant by the difference in method is not so easy to guess. Structurally, *The Wild Duck* hardly deviates from Ibsen's other realistic plays, except that it is woven of a more ordinary everyday material than any of his earlier works. Where it differs though, and most radically, is in that attitude towards man and life with which he imbued the whole play. His pessimism in *Ghosts*, for instance, was still rebellious and indignant. Here it is one of contempt.

Yet, as after *Emperor and Galilean*, Ibsen the dramatist, the seeker and the fighter, could not afford to remain stuck in a blind-alley from which there was no outlet in any direction. On this occasion, the outlet was provided by his own individualism, which made him turn from the average to the exceptions, and pin his hopes on those few aristocrats of mind and spirit who are made of finer material than all sorts of Hialmar Ekdals. Such a change was bound to shift his attention entirely to the workings of individual consciousness in its contest with the destructive powers inside as well as outside itself. This brought him, however, face to face with new conflicts and dilemmas, beginning with his *Rosmersholm*.

X

THE 'INSECURITY OF CONSCIENCE'

I

ROSMERSHOLM is a tragedy of over-sensitive conscience, depicted against the background of political passions and party-struggles as witnessed by Ibsen during his summer holidays in his native country in 1885. This was his second visit, since his departure in 1864, to Norway, and the internal political squabbles by which she was torn at the time left an unpleasant taste in his mouth—as though he had been watching a fight between 'two million cats and dogs'. Ibsen had never been an admirer of politics and politicians, partly because he was convinced that the methods used by them could not but contaminate the progressive democratic movement in Europe and turn it into a process of general plebeianization. This only made him wish the more fervently that an 'element of nobility should be introduced into our political life, our government, our representative bodies, and our press', as he put it in his talk to the workers at Trondheim on June 14th, 1885. 'I do not mean, of course, the nobility of birth, of money, of science, or even of gifts and talents, but the nobility of character, of will and thought.'

Something of this aristo-democracy was behind the dreams and ideas of the ex-Pastor Johannes Rosmer—the hero of Ibsen's new play. Like Ibsen himself, Rosmer had been brought up in an atmosphere of pietistic Protestant mentality, the influence of which he could not shake off even after he had given up all his inherited religious convictions. He was, moreover, steeped in the traditions of his noble ancestors, whose integrity had always been matched only by their gloomy outlook upon life and the world. Such things as joy and laughter were unknown to them. Something of their gloom actually seems to have infected the entire countryside. His ancestral Rosmersholm was haunted, from time to time, by weird apparitions (the ghostly white horses), and the landscape around was enough to remind one of our earth being a 'vale of tears'. Rosmer was the first of his kin to rebel against that sullenness. But in doing this, he still retained all the high ethical views and values bequeathed to him by his ancestors. The voice of moral responsibility became even stronger in him after he had exchanged his coldly relentless Christian faith for the freer outlook then in vogue.

As he wished to realize himself through a full and active life, he embraced a new task which offered him the widest possible scope in this direction. It was by no means the one-sided puritanic path of Brand by which he hoped to reach his goal. Like the artist Oswald in *Ghosts*, he dreamt of combining his vocation with joy, light and sunshine, and with radiant happiness. It is significant that in the early drafts of the play Rosmer is intent primarily on escaping from the inherited gloom with its Calvinistic guilt-complex (or 'insecurity of conscience') which, like a dead weight, had hung over him all the time. As though awakening from a nightmare on a bright summer morning, he exclaims:

'All around, in every department of life, a luxurious germination is going on. And it is time I too began to live. I must and will be happy in this world.'
'It is in the air. It is one of the greatest things about the new age that we dare openly proclaim happiness as our end in life.'

These words are added by Miss Dankett (Rebecca West in the final version of the play), whose moral complexion is entirely different from that of Rosmer.

But Rosmer's respectable brother-in-law and the local 'pillar of society', Gylling (Rector Kroll in the play), breaks in with the remark which anticipates the tragedy of both Rosmer and Rebecca:

'Poor man, you with your conscience burdened with guilt—you think you can find happiness by those devious paths. You are founding your happiness on water.'

II

Gylling knew what he was talking about. For behind his words there was an allusion to the suicide of Rosmer's wife, Beata, the real cause of which was still a mystery and a matter of conjecture. It weighed heavily on Rosmer himself, although he was not responsible—not wittingly responsible—for it. But since the fact of her suicide was there, its secret *had* to be unravelled for the sake of his own conscience and peace of mind. The more so because he felt that his dead wife was like a 'corpse on his back'—now that, having emancipated himself from his old views, he wanted to turn all his thoughts towards joy and happiness. The whole of this drama is largely a struggle between Rosmer and the 'corpse on his back'. It even goes deeper than that. As though commenting upon Rosmer's own state of mind after a series of shocks and disappointments, his one-time tutor, Hetman (Ulrik Brendel in the play), who has also been mauled in his attempt to realize himself through active life, complains bitterly:

'It is all rubbish, my boy. Empty dreams. Nothing but mocking shadows. Humanity is past help. . . . The Master feels there is a flaw in the work. And he takes a firm stand. Insecurity of conscience, my boy. And that is what we have all inherited. That is why humanity is incurable. Past help.'

'Then is life worth living?' [asks Miss Dankett].

'Oh, yes. Only avoid doing silly things. No quackery. Let life swing right or left—just as it chances.'

'But one's self. Each individual?'

'Eat, drink and be merry, my fair young lady. And you must take existence in the same way, Rosmer. The Master forgot to give us wings. Both inner and outer ones. So let us crawl on the earth as long as we can. There is nothing else to be done.'

But this precisely is the advice which Rosmer, or for that matter Hetman (Brendel) himself, could never have followed. It is all right to recommend such alternatives to people with a coarse moral constitution. For them it is easy to run away from themselves—in the manner of Peer Gynt—into those dissipations and 'enjoyments' which are the very negation of true joy. A person with Rosmer's sensitiveness, however, could hardly contemplate anything of this kind. He is morally much too awakened and too aware of what he is doing. Hence his vulnerability. He either must face and overcome his ever-present sense of guilt, or else bear the consequences of his own failure.

Such at any rate is his dilemma. In spite of his new aims and intentions—the intentions of an intellectually emancipated man—the irrational side in him, his 'insecure conscience', proves in the end stronger. The tragic impact of the play is increased by the fate of Rebecca, who soon becomes even more important than Rosmer. Yet by transferring the centre of gravity to her, Ibsen complicated —both psychologically and morally—the inner drama of Rosmer himself.

III

When Rebecca came to Rosmer's house, she was like the sea element of her native North—a natural force rather than a tamed human being. Devoid of any conscience, but with an attitude towards life that was amoral (or pre-moral) rather than immoral, she formed a complete contrast to Rosmer. Nor had her background anything in common with his. She was the illegitimate child of a doctor—a notorious roué; and according to a hint from her she must have had intimate relations even with her own father. But questions of good and evil, or scruples of any kind, did not worry her in those days. There was no rift in her will, which seemed to be all of a piece and refused to see any obstacles standing in the way of her indomitable vitality.

With a disposition such as this, she came to Rosmer's house in order to look after his sick wife Beata. Soon, however, Rebecca fell in love with Rosmer and, true to her own nature, made a plan to oust Beata by fair means or foul. It did not take long before her crisp up-to-date intellect made due impression upon Rosmer. This was what she had aimed at. Having decided to 'emancipate' the rather conservative Pastor by destroying all his inherited views and beliefs, she was sure sooner or later to undermine also that moral fastidiousness of his which stood in the way of their union. At the same time she succeeded in winning the sympathies of the hysterical, over-sexed Beata who became fascinated by her to the pitch of adoration. Beata was painfully aware of the fact that her own state of health alienated her physically from her husband. Hence Rebecca found it all the easier to make her think that her own relations with Johannes Rosmer were more serious than just ordinary friendship. She even pretended to expect a child as a result of what was supposed to be their secret love.

Rosmer had not the remotest idea of the intrigue that was going on behind his back. Nor did it ever enter his head to deceive his wife, to whom he remained absolutely loyal—love or no love. Rebecca, on the other hand, knew what she wanted, and her calculations proved right: the distracted and cruelly misled Beata obliged her by committing suicide in the adjoining mill-race. All the obstacles were thus removed. Rebecca could not but feel that Rosmer, too, was attached to her and needed her companionship, especially after Beata's death. Yet when the path was clear; when everything seemed to point to the possibility of a married union between the two, something strange happened: Rebecca suddenly discovered that she was farther away from her goal than at the beginning. There were no external reasons why this should be so; the change came exclusively from within.

It is true that under the sway of Rebecca's influence, Rosmer had adopted her radical modern views and ideas. What remained unchanged in him, though, was his inherited moral sense. Far from turning him into an irresponsible rake (in the style of Rebecca's father), the loss of his old faith brought out even more potently the innate nobility of his character. It also made him yearn for a life broad enough to free him entirely of his former Protestant despondency. That was why he saw his new task or mission in spreading the same kind of inner nobility and joy all over the country. He wanted to 'go as a messenger from home to home; to win over minds and wills; to create noblemen in wider and wider circles. Joyful noblemen. For it is joy that ennobles the mind.' The only thing that kept disturbing this prospective calling of his was the puzzle of Beata's death. He was sure that Beata, with her unbalanced mind, must have misinterpreted his friendship for Rebecca in a sense which drove her to suicide from jealousy. The mere probability of such an indirect guilt was enough to stir up Rosmer's conscience and to threaten him with frustration just when he was about to launch his gospel of a joyful and noble life.

'There will always be a doubt—a question left. I can never again revel in that which makes life so marvellously sweet to live.'
'What is it you mean, Rosmer?'
'Peaceful, happy innocence!'

His 'insecurity of conscience' thus began playing havoc with him at a time he could least afford it. He now had before him a definite task which he wanted to combine with the greatest joy and happiness accessible to man, yet his feeling of guilt barred him the way. At last he saw an outlet—in marrying Rebecca. He was sure that in this case Beata would be 'completely out of the saga for ever and ever. . . . It must be so! It must! I cannot—I will not go through life with a corpse on my back. Help me to cast it off, Rebecca. And let us stifle all memories in freedom, in joy, in passion. You shall be the only wife I have ever had.'

IV

One would expect rapturous consent from her, but nothing of the sort happens. She utters a cry of joy, but in a moment masters her emotion and tells him, with something like fright, yet firmly, that on no account could she ever marry him. Bit by bit, and with intervals full of suspense, Ibsen makes Rebecca disclose the history of the inner process responsible for her strange and unexpected refusal.

It transpires that while she was so persistently influencing Rosmer's mind, she herself came under the spell of his moral nobility, which infected—by stealth as it were—her heart and gradually undermined her will. Before she was aware of what exactly had happened, her conscience had awakened and made her bow to a law which was stronger than all her will-power. She herself could not understand the change within her, yet the change was there—irrevocable and powerful enough to make her confess to Rosmer her guilt in Beata's death. And together with this also the price she had had to pay for her own regeneration:

Rosmersholm has broken me. Broken me utterly and hopelessly. I had a fresh, undaunted will when I came here. Now I have bent my neck under a strange law. . . . I believe I could have accomplished anything—at that time. For I still had my undaunted, free-born will. I knew no scruples—I stood in awe of no human relation. But then began what has broken down my will, and cowed me so piteously for my whole life. Rosmersholm has sapped my strength. My old undaunted will has had its wings clipped here. It is crippled! The time is past when I had courage for anything in the world. I have lost the power of action, Rosmer. . . . When I found myself sharing your life here—in quiet—in solitude—when you showed me all your thoughts without reserve—every tender and delicate feeling, just as it came to you—then the great change came over me. Little by little, you understand. Almost imperceptibly—but at last with such overwhelming force that it reached to the depths of my soul. . . . All the rest—the horrible sense-intoxicated desire—passed far, far away from me. All the whirling passion settled down into quiet and silence. Rest descended on my soul—a stillness as one on our northern bird-cliffs under the midnight sun. . . . It was love that was born in me. The great self-denying love, that is content with life, as we two have lived it together. . . . Yesterday—when you asked me if I could be your wife—I cried out with joy! For a moment, yes, I had forgotten myself. It was my old buoyant will that was struggling

to be free. But it has no energy left now—no power of endurance. . . .
It is the Rosmer view of life—or your view of life, at any rate—that has
infected my will. And made it sick. Enslaved it to laws that had no
power over me before. You—life with you—has ennobled my mind.
You may safely believe it! The Rosmer view of life ennobles. But—but
it kills happiness. My happiness, at any rate. . . . Yes, Rosmer—this is
the terrible part of it: that now, when all life's happiness is within my
grasp—my heart is changed, and my own past cuts me off from it.

It should be remembered that before listening to Rebecca's
confession, Rosmer had passed through a crushing experience
which proved to him once and for all the *naïveté* of his attempts
to ennoble human beings from without. This increases his
need of Rebecca. He feels utterly defeated, and but for her he
may fall a prey to loneliness and despair. Afraid of what might
happen once she has left him—and after her confession there is
no other alternative—he tries to persuade her to stay, while yet in
the grip of the darkest doubts.

ROSMER: Your past is dead, Rebecca. It has no hold on you any more
—it is no part of you—as you are *now*.
REBECCA: Oh, you know that these are only phrases, dear. And innocence? Where am I to get that from? Yes, innocence. That is the source
of peace and happiness. That was the vital truth you were to implant in
the coming generation of happy noble-men——
ROSMER: Oh, don't remind me of that. It was only an abortive dream,
Rebecca—an immature idea, that I myself no longer believe in.—Ah, no,
we cannot be ennobled from without.
REBECCA (*softly*): Not even by tranquil love, Rosmer?
ROSMER (*thoughtfully*): Yes—that would be the great thing—the most
glorious in life, almost—if it were so. (*Moves uneasily.*) But how can I
be certain of that? How convince myself?
REBECCA: Do you not believe me, Rosmer?

But once assailed by his doubt, Rosmer can no longer shake it
off. He believes neither in himself nor in Rebecca, and even less
in his power to transform his fellow-beings, and he says so.
Rebecca insists on the fact that he has transformed at least one
human being—herself. But this is not enough to resuscitate
Rosmer's faith in himself and in life.

REBECCA (*looks darkly at him*): Then how will you be able to live your
life?

ROSMER: That I don't know. I don't understand how. I don't think I *can* live it. And I know nothing in the world that is worth living for.

REBECCA: Oh, life—life will renew itself. Let us hold fast to it, Rosmer. We shall leave it soon enough.

ROSMER (*springs up restlessly*): Then give me my faith again! My faith in you, Rebecca. My faith in your love! Proof! I must have proof!

REBECCA: Proof? How can I give you proof?

ROSMER: You must! (*Walks across the room.*) I cannot bear this desolation—this horrible emptiness—this—this——

Here a loud knock startles them, and that eccentric, Ulrik Brendel, returns from his own attempt to ennoble other fellow-beings. He, too, is as heavily defeated in his own way as Rosmer is in his. From this moment on, the dénouement assumes a course which becomes inevitable for both Rosmer and Rebecca.

V

The frustration of Rosmer's 'mission' had much to do with the party intrigues and party struggles that were raging in Norway at the time. As it happened, the bosses of the losing conservatives in Rosmer's district wanted to entice—for opportunist reasons—Rosmer himself into their fold. But since Rosmer's new outlook would not allow him to join them, they used blackmail, intimidation and even dirty allusions to the supposed 'liaison' between Rebecca and him in order to achieve their object. Crushed by Rebecca's first confession, Rosmer thought for a while of joining Kroll and his political companions; but these convinced him at once that politics in our brave new world have nothing to do with nobility of any kind. It was during the same political campaign that Ulrik Brendel, anxious to fight for a better future, had joined the President of the local radicals, Peter Mortensgaard. But he, too, had to learn his lesson. In the dead of night, while Rebecca was waiting for the steamer to take her away from Rosmersholm for ever, he came again to Johannes Rosmer—this time with the object of borrowing from him 'one or two cast off ideals'.

BRENDEL: For I am cleaned out, my boy. Ruined, beggared. . . . For five-and-twenty years I have sat like a miser on his double-locked treasure-chest. And then yesterday—when I open it and want to display the treasure—there's none there! The teeth of time had ground it into dust. There was *Nichts* and nothing in the whole concern.'

ROSMER: But are you sure of that?

BRENDEL: There's no room for doubt, my dear fellow. The President has convinced me of it. . . . Peter Mortensgaard, of course . . . (*mysteriously.*) Hush, hush, hush! Peter Mortensgaard is the lord and leader of the future. Never have I stood in a more august presence. Peter Mortensgaard has the secret of omnipotence. He can do whatever he will. . . . Yes, yes, my boy! For Peter Mortensgaard never wills more than he can do. Peter Mortensgaard is capable of living his life without ideals. And that, you see—that is just the mighty secret of action and of victory. It is the sum of the whole world's wisdom. *Basta!*

ROSMER (*in a low voice*): Now I understand—why you leave here poorer than you came.

BRENDEL: *Bien!* then take a *Beispiel* by your old teacher. Rub out all that he once imprinted on your mind. Build not thy house on shifting sand. And look ahead—and feel your way—before you build on this exquisite creature, who here lends sweetness to your life.

REBECCA: Why I am not to be built on?

BRENDEL (*comes a step nearer*): I gather that my former pupil has a great cause to carry forward to victory.

REBECCA: And if so——?

BRENDEL: Victory is sure. But—mark me well—on one inevitable condition.

REBECCA: Which is——?

BRENDEL (*takes her gently by the wrist*): That the woman who loves him shall gladly go out into the kitchen and hack her tender, rosy-white little finger—*here*—just *here* in the middle point. Item, that the aforesaid loving woman—again gladly—shall slice off her incomparably moulded left ear (*lets her go and turns to Rosmer*). Farewell, my conquering Johannes.

ROSMER: Are you going now? In the dark night?

BRENDEL: The dark night is best. Peace be with you. (*He goes.*)

(*There is a short silence in the room.*)

REBECCA (*breathes heavily*): Oh, how close and sultry it is here! (*Goes to the window, opens, and remains standing by it.*)

ROSMER (*sits down in the arm-chair by the stove*): There's nothing else for it after all, Rebecca. I see it. You must go away.

REBECCA: Yes, I see no choice.

Aware of Rosmer's own 'pitiful lamentable defeat', Rebecca cannot go away, though, without trying to resuscitate his former belief in himself and in his calling. After all, he had already ennobled one human being—herself—for the rest of her life. Was not that a sufficient proof? But her words, instead of convincing him, only deepen his despair, until—under its impact—all the pathological egoism of Rosmer's weakness (strengthened by his unconscious death-wish) comes out. At first he only toys with the 'horrible fascination' of the idea of sacrifice and is reluctant even to mention it to Rebecca. In the end, however, he suggests to her the only proof that would convince him: her willingness to go 'gladly, as Ulrik Brendel said', the same way that Beata went.* Rebecca is at first voiceless with surprise. On coming to herself, she asks him what would happen if she had the heart to do it willingly and gladly.

ROSMER: I should have to believe you then. I should recover my faith in my mission. Faith in my power to ennoble human souls. Faith in the human soul's power to attain nobility.

REBECCA (*takes up her shawl slowly, and puts it over her head: says with composure*): You shall have your faith again.

Rosmer realizes the madness of it all, but is unable to resist its 'fascination'. Anyway, he knows full well that whatever Rebecca does or does not do, his own life is finished. So there is no use pretending that it can be patched up, or that any sacrifice would save him from desolation. On seeing Rebecca's seriousness, he regains his composure, but it is too late: for she is now determined to go Beata's way not only for his sake, but also in order to atone for her own past guilt. 'What I have sinned—it is fit that I should expiate.'

ROSMER (*looks at her fixedly*): Is that your point of view?
REBECCA: Yes.
ROSMER (*with resolution*): Well then, I stand firm in our emancipated view of life, Rebecca. There is no judge over us; and therefore we must do justice upon ourselves.
REBECCA (*misunderstanding him*): Yes, that is true—that too. My going away will save what is best in you.
ROSMER: Oh, there is nothing left to save in me.
REBECCA: Yes, there is, but I—after to-day, I should only be a sea-troll dragging down the ship that is to carry you forward. I must go overboard. Why should I remain here in the world, trailing after me my own crippled life? Why brood and brood over the happiness that my past has forfeited for ever? I must give up the game, Rosmer.
ROSMER: If you go—I go with you.

* This is one of those passages in which Ibsen leaves almost too much to the actor, because when read it strikes one as being much too unexpected and not sufficiently motivated psychologically, that is not quite in agreement with Rosmer's previous character.

Since they cannot be united in life, the two can still become one in death. Inseparable as man and wife, they plunge into the same mill-race which had once engulfed the cunningly deluded Beata.

If the end of *Ghosts* was pessimistic, the finale of *Rosmersholm* is tragic; because its catastrophe is at the same time also a triumph. On the plane of ordinary common sense Rebecca's and Rosmer's end may strike one as being sheer romantic lunacy. But it can also stir in us certain springs, which testify to man's potential nobility even in defeat and despair. Ibsen's explorings of individual consciousness did not stop here, though. He continued them, on various levels, in *The Lady from the Sea*, *Hedda Gabler*, and *The Master Builder*.

XI

THE LAW OF ADJUSTMENT

I

*T*HE *Lady from the Sea* and *Hedda Gabler* deal with feminine
psychology in married life from two different angles and with
different results. The problem in both plays is one of individual
adjustment, treated by Ibsen not only with consummate tact but
also with unusual detachment. In *The Lady from the Sea* he
touches moreover upon the subconscious in terms of psycho-
analytical images, which are obviously less baffling to present-day
audiences than they were to his contemporaries.

Ellida Wangel, the 'lady from the sea', suffers from an acute
anxiety-neurosis. She, too, like Rebecca in *Rosmersholm* (but in a
much more inhibited form), is under the spell of the sea-element—
a symbol of the anarchic 'freedom' let loose in man's psyche. The
whole play is in essence a dramatized history of her cure by the
method of sublimation—long before this word became vulgarized
by the jargon of modern psychology. Sexually maladjusted to her
much older husband, Dr. Wangel—a widower, whom she had
married without really loving, she cannot 'acclimatize' herself
and, therefore, feels a stranger to him, to her two step-daughters
Boletta and Hilda; in fact, to all her inland surroundings, so
different from her sea-battered native shore in the North. She is
like a mermaid thrown by the waves on to the beach, and unable
either to go back to the sea, or to get accustomed to dry land.

But there are other purely irrational complications as well.
As a young girl, Ellida had been so much attracted by a roaming
Finnish sailor that she became his fiancée, with the sea as the only
witness of their betrothal and at the same time the receptacle of
their wedding rings. The sailor departed, but his spell—identical
with that of the sea—persisted and grew stronger after she had
'sold' herself to Dr. Wangel and settled far inland. The child born
of that marriage had her seaman's eyes, and the infant's sudden
death aggravated Ellida's state of nerves to the extent of making
her discontinue marital intercourse with her husband. The fixed
idea that in her deepest self she still belonged to the seaman

became an obsession she could not shake off, however much she
wanted at times to be 'saved from herself'. In order to alleviate her
trouble, Dr. Wangel proposed to take her for a while back to the
'salt-laden, sweeping sea-breezes' of her native North, but she
would not hear of it.

'Oh, do not speak of it! Don't think of such a thing! There is no help
for me in that! I know, I feel, that I should not be able to throw it off
out there either.'

'To throw it off, dear? What do you mean?'

'I mean the terror of him. His unfathomable power over me.'

II

By expedients of his own, Dr. Wangel makes Ellida tell him all
about her past adventure with the sea-stranger, as well as her
nervous and in a large measure telepathic anticipation of his
return. Unable to discard the notion that her marriage to Dr.
Wangel was a kind of betrayal, she is sure that the return of the
sea-man will impose upon her a final choice between him and her
present husband. But such moods and fancies only increase her
nervous trouble, while her atavistic kinship with the sea, with its
mysterious wild freedom, makes her rebel all the more against her
inland existence. This unconscious rebellion against her husband
becomes intensified as the return of the Stranger—after years of
absence—unavoidably draws near. The very words she hurls at
Dr. Wangel vibrate with her longing for the freedom she must have
known in the past.

'I know you can keep me here. You have the power, and, no doubt,
you will use it! But my mind—all my thoughts—all my irresistible
longings and desires—these you cannot fetter! They will yearn and
strain—out into the Unknown—that I was created for—and that you
have barred against me.'

But her doctor-husband has no intention of using force or of
barring anything against her. On the contrary, he tries to quieten
her nerves as far as possible by inducing her to find out and to
confess (in an almost psycho-analytical manner) the deeper roots
and causes of her trouble. And when the Stranger actually appears, her husband's curative method remains one of freedom.
This alone makes Ellida waver in her dilemma of choosing between
the two men. The first thing that turns the situation in favour of

Dr. Wangel is the Stranger's changed appearance—so different from the mental image cherished by Ellida during the years of his absence. She does not even recognize him at first, except by his eyes. A more important factor is, however, the liberty of choice which, at the crucial moment, Dr. Wangel grants her at the risk of losing her for ever.

'Now you are wholly free from me and mine. Now your own true life can return to its—its right groove again. For now you can choose in freedom and on your own responsibility.'

To her surprise she discovers that being free to choose, she is also free to reject—on her own responsibility, that is, as an independent individual. The Stranger's spell over Ellida weakens. Her final choice falls on her husband, and the dangers that threatened her from the depths of her Unconscious are over. Acclimatization to her surroundings promises to be an easier task from now on. Adapting herself to the circumstances in order to adapt them to herself, she is on the way towards realizing what is best in her both as wife and human being.

'I begin to understand you—by degrees,' [her husband comments after all the trials endured.] 'You think and conceive in images—in visible pictures. Your longing and yearning for the sea—the fascination that he—the stranger possessed for you—have been the expression of an awakening and growing need for freedom within you—nothing else.'

'Oh, I don't know what to say to that. But you have been a good physician for me. You found—and you had the courage to use—the right remedy—the only one that could help me.'

All the minor characters in the play are grouped in such a manner as to balance and complete its pattern. In marrying the much older schoolmaster, Arnholm, whom she does not really love, Boletta seems to repeat Ellida's own mistake, with a similar crisis probably awaiting her some time in the future. The capricious impish Hilda is passing through the fermenting period of girlhood in order to emerge in an entirely new rôle in *The Master Builder*. The consumptive artist Lyngstrand is an *ingénu* whose egoism willy-nilly parodies the problem of inspiring love: the Falk-Svanhild motif in *Love's Comedy*. The ubiquitous Ballested again represents a parody of adjustment. He is a man who mechanically 'acclimatizes' himself to any circumstances as their passive tool, not as their master.

The Lady from the Sea is, in some respects, a more or less hopeful corrective to The Wild Duck, although its serenity is that of a declining autumn day. Ellida and Wangel are of a much higher calibre than Gina and Hialmar Ekdal, but they still belong to average humanity, and their mutual adjustment points towards something that is of a bigger and more general import. There is even a certain connection between Ellida and Nora at the end of A Doll's House. The 'miracle of miracles' of a perfectly adjusted marriage, hinted at by Nora in her parting words to Helmer, is achieved by Ellida and her husband, both of whom can thus fulfil their destinies, no matter how modest their actual status in life may be. The deeper meaning of Ellida's 'acclimatization' consists in her willingness to accept henceforth her daily duties in a spirit which is likely to take away all their tediousness. Certain implications of this play can, however, best be understood if Ellida's fate is compared with that of Hedda in Hedda Gabler—another drama of maladjustment, but from a different angle.

III

Hedda Gabler has puzzled many a critic, let alone ordinary readers. One of Ibsen's commentators (Lothar) even sees in it a modernist parody of The Vikings in Helgeland. Hedda is likened by him to an up-to-date Hjördis gone to seed. Hjördis's good-natured but stupid husband, Gunnar, corresponds to Tesman; Sigurd to Eilert Lövborg; and Agny to Thea Elvsted. All this may sound plausible, but it takes us nowhere. True enough, Ibsen did not mind repeating similar characters and situations, but only when he could thereby express something new. And Hedda Gabler is full of new things, beginning with the heroine herself—one of the most memorable and at the same time 'decadent' portraits ever shaped by him. Her maladjusted marriage is definitely tainted with the fin de siècle; and the atmosphere which pervades it is, in contrast to The Lady from the Sea, that of a complete cul-de-sac.

Having endured agonies of boredom on her long honeymoon-journey (during which her husband, Jörgen Tesman—a narrow-minded pedant—was collecting materials for a thesis on medieval domestic crafts in Brabant), Hedda feels no less bored on her return to Christiania. An impoverished child of the privileged upper set with military traditions, she is spiteful towards her hopelessly mediocre husband; his recently acquired suburban villa—so redolent of middle-class respectability; his kind-hearted aunt; and even towards her own incipient pregnancy which fills her with disgust rather than with the joy of prospective motherhood. Like Ellida, she seems to be created for life on a bigger scale. There is in her a secret longing for beauty, for freedom and *élan*; but all this was sapped by prejudices and class-conventions even before she could spread out her wings. Her energies had thus turned sour. What was potentially good in her, became distorted and even perverted. Her love of beauty, for example, degenerated into a priggish 'aesthetic' pose; and her repressed wish for a broader existence eventually descended to envious peeping (as if through a keyhole) into the doings of those who, like Lövborg, were reckless enough to be themselves and to live their own lives at least in a negative sense. While devoid of any moral standards, she is yet hide-bound by the rules of 'this is done' and 'this is not done', behind which there is nothing but a vacuum. It is not morality, but her fear of scandal that makes her resist even a *liaison* with the slick Assessor Brack—surely an expert in family triangles.

There was a time in Hedda's past when she had felt something like love for the promising young scholar (and Tesman's comrade) Eilert Lövborg. She chased him away, though, without mercy, once his scandalous life made him no longer acceptable in society. But now one of the first things Hedda learns to her surprise, when back again in Christiania, is that Lövborg, too, happens to be in town—a reformed character and author of a much discussed book on civilization. It transpires that such a change in his life was due to an old acquaintance of Hedda's: a certain Thea Elvsted who, in the wilds of the countryside, helped Lövborg to find his feet and become worthy of his gifts. But as she was not quite sure of his power to resist the temptations of city life, Thea, in defiance of all conventions, left her husband and followed Lövborg right to the capital. She even called on the Tesmans with the request that they should receive him with kindness, should he pay them a visit.

Astir with curiosity, Hedda remains outwardly calm and self-possessed as ever. With her usual adroitness, she extracts from Thea all the details she needs. But here Lövborg himself calls and is duly welcomed. His visit marks the beginning of a double tragedy: that of Hedda and of Lövborg.

IV

Envious of Thea's influence on such an extraordinary man, and not a little jealous, Hedda suddenly decides to try her own power over her one-time admirer. An opportunity arises on the spot. With diabolical cunning she insinuates that Thea's presence in the capital is due to her lack of faith in Lövborg—a thing which Lövborg immediately resents. Hedda herself pretends to have a higher opinion of his strength. In order to prove her own faith in him, she bids him join one of those 'most lively' parties at Assessor Brack's which seem to be suitable for bachelors of a certain type. As though defying Thea's doubts, Lövborg goes to the party. But the test is too much for him. Far from triumphing over his former weaknesses, he gets thoroughly drunk. He does not return with 'vine-leaves round his head', as Hedda expected him to do, but goes to a disreputable woman's flat instead. On the way he loses the MS. of the sequel of his famous book (he had promised to read it to Tesman), and the end of it all is a scandalous row with the police.

Lövborg finds himself once again beyond the pale of society, and this time for good. Thea's pathetic despair of a mother whose child has come to grief, is well contrasted with the contemptuous calm of Hedda. Resentful because of her defeat, Hedda is still jealous of Thea and does not refrain even from callously burning Lövborg's MS., before Tesman, who has found it on his way home, is able to intervene. Her composure remains the same when Lövborg himself comes to say good-bye. He knows that socially he is now finished. And so does she. But instead of reproaching him, she only hands him one of her late father's pistols—with the tacit injunction that he should at least die with dignity.

Once again everything goes wrong. Lövborg does not commit suicide with the dignified ritual of a samurai, but is mortally wounded in the stomach—during a quarrel with the prostitute, whom he has wrongly suspected of having stolen his MS. To make things worse, Assessor Brack recognizes the pistol as being one of Hedda's, and the price demanded by him for silence (which alone will save her from being involved in a disgusting 'scandal') is nothing less than the hoped-for triangle as a certainty. Hedda, however, rebels when she is least expected to do so. Her freedom may be empty enough, yet she asserts it in her own way at the moment Brack is almost sure of victory. While Tesman is helping to reconstruct Lövborg's MS. from the jottings preserved by Thea, a shot resounds in the adjoining room, and Hedda is no more.

v

Ibsen's Hedda—that 'Valkyrie in a corset', as one of his critics called her—is a study in frustration. In contrast to Ellida in *The Lady from the Sea*, she is not only unable, but also unwilling, to 'acclimatize' herself creatively to life. Hence she finds no place in it. Her marriage is something unreal and casual—much too casual even to become a problem. It is only a convenient shelter for a decadent *fin de siècle* woman, doomed to be a victim of her own futility and boredom. But she also embodies the tragedy of potential strength which becomes destructive for lack of a proper outlet. 'Hedda's despair is that there are, doubtless, so many chances in the world, but she cannot discover them,' we read in Ibsen's notes to the play. 'It is the want of an object in life that torments her.' In her priggish and isolated hot-house existence, she is devoid of any task in the name of which she could realize herself. Hence her continuous inner and external vacuum, until she puts an end to it all.

Hedda Gabler and *The Lady from the Sea* approach the dilemma of one's adjustment to life from the two opposite yet complementary ends—complementary because of their very contrasts. But as usual, Ibsen could not and did not stop here. He transferred his attention to a truly creative individual who has found his 'object', his mission in life, and has yet failed—though in a manner different from Hedda's. This brings us to one of Ibsen's most puzzling plays, *The Master Builder*.

XII

THE MASTER-BUILDER'S DOWNFALL

I

WHEREAS *Hedda Gabler* is extremely detached as a work of art, *The Master Builder* can justly be called a personal confession in disguise. At the age of sixty-four and at the height of his fame, Ibsen held in this work a 'doomsday' over himself by assessing his previous endeavours, aspirations, victories and defeats. One is not far wrong in seeing in the master-builder Solness Ibsen's own double. Solness, like Ibsen, was a self-made man, who after a hard struggle had succeeded in his particular calling and had acquired both wealth and fame. Like Ibsen again, Solness was apprehensive of the younger generation. It is known that after his return to Norway Ibsen listened with considerable interest to the voices of the young authors. One of them, Knut Hamsun, who was not exactly well disposed towards him, soon emerged as a talent of international reputation. Even the course of Solness's career, as has often been pointed out, is analogous with the three stages of Ibsen's own development. Solness, who first built churches, then ordinary human houses, and finally dwellings with towers pointing to the 'dizzy heights', resembles Ibsen, whose work had to pass through something similar during his romantic, realistic, and symbolist periods. Moreover, the Master-Builder's love for young Hilda Wangel reflects Ibsen's own affection for a seventeen years old Viennese girl—Emilie Bardach—whom he met in the summer of 1889 at Gossensass in Tyrol. He actually called her, on a photo he presented her with, the May-sun of his September-life (*die Maisonne eines Septemberlebens*).

The deeper inner impact of that acquaintanceship may have been partly responsible for the genesis of *The Master Builder*. It would be far-fetched, though, to interpret it in the light of a love-affair between Ibsen who was in his seventh decade and the temperamental Viennese flapper—still in her teens. In spite of one of Emilie's strange entries in her diary to the effect that the aged dramatist wanted to be more to her than a friend or a mere platonic lover, one is inclined to accept Ibsen's own assertion, when referring to that idyll, that he had made use of Emilie only for his art—as a 'model' for his play.* This does not exclude, of course, the coincidence of certain minor misunderstandings and frictions in his married life, which probably made him take his episode with Emilie Bardach more seriously at times—according to his moods. In his biography of Ibsen, A. E. Zucker relates how Emilie herself told him (during an interview) that the aged dramatist had spoken in those days of a possible divorce, after which he would marry her and undertake wide travels to show her the world.

Whatever the truth, the whole of that adventure, with its actual or possible implications, is still baffling enough, but less so than the drama it inspired. The first impression of *The Master Builder* is one of an elusiveness which defies all our notions of probability. Neither its plot nor its dialogue is thinkable on the plane of our everyday existence. As a projection of a creator's tragic inner experience it becomes, however, highly convincing—provided we have the right key to it. For practically each sentence seems to have a meaning beyond its face value. In this case, the key ought to be sought in the hidden inner conflict of Ibsen himself. The play may not be realistic in the usual sense of this word; yet in a deeper spiritual sense it is profoundly real, and this is after all what matters.

II

The master-builder Solness, unlike so many of Ibsen's characters, cannot say that he had been frustrated in his vocation. He was fortunate enough to have found early enough that life-task which gave an outlet to his talent and ambitions. He was thus able to realize himself through his calling. Yet something must have gone wrong in spite of that, because every step he made forward had to be paid for by some heavy sacrifice which brought him in the end nothing but suffering. The price demanded was the loss of happiness—not his personal happiness only, but that of other human beings as well. His very start was due to the fire which had gutted his wife's ancestral home, and had also caused the death of his two children. From that time on the road to success was open to him, while his wife Aline was thwarted in her maternal vocation, and consequently could not find her place in life. Instead of living

* Reference to the diary can be found in A. E. Zucker's books.

in the present, she was chained to the past—to the toys and shadows of her childless nursery. Solness had made enormous strides in his calling, but there was no real joy in it—only work and sacrifice. Nor was there any promise of joy in the future.

'All that I have succeeded in doing, building, creating—oh, isn't it terrible even to think of——! That all this I have to make up for—not in money, but in human happiness. And not with my own happiness only, but with other people's too. That is the price which my position as an artist has cost me—and others. And every single day I have to look on while the price is paid for me anew. Over again—and over again for ever.'

Like so many people who have had to struggle hard in order to satisfy their ambitions, the Master-Builder, having reached the height of success, is jealous of any talented young rivals 'knocking at the door'. It is fear that makes him keep young Ragnar (whose architect-father, Knut Brovik, has also been frustrated by him) in a subordinate position. He is doing his best to curb him by tricks and methods he himself hates, but cannot help. Nor can he help commiting further hateful deeds which make him and other people suffer. For he acts as though urged by some irrational power which he is unable to fathom. This is why he compares the whole of his externally successful vocation with a sore on his breast. His mysterious 'servers and helpers' flay other people alive in order to heal that sore, but it can never be healed, and he knows it. Hence his feeling of guilt; and also his fear of the retribution which he expects to come—perhaps in the shape of revenge on the part of the dreaded younger generation. But when the latter, in the person of Hilda Wangel, actually knocks at his door, his fears are allayed: instead of being pushed aside, he finds in Hilda the source of renewed inspiration he has been secretly craving for all along, and is spurred on by her to the highest creative ascent of which he is still capable.

III

There is something of Rebecca's vitality in Hilda Wangel. She is her healthy counterpart, though, devoid of hardness and perversity, and entirely under the sway of her own romantic dreaming. In contrast to the Master-Builder's wife Aline, who walks about like an animated mummy and lives in the past, Hilda comes in like a breezy wind from the future. As a little girl she had been thrilled by Solness when seeing him high up on a newly-built church-tower, where—cheered by the crowd below—he hung the customary wreath on the steeple. 'Oh, it was so gloriously thrilling. I could not have believed there was a builder in the whole world that could build such a tremendously high tower. And then that you yourself should stand at the very top of it, as large as life! And that you should not be the least bit dizzy! It was that above everything that made one—made one dizzy to think of.' When standing so high, the Master-Builder was apparently hurling some words into the sky, as though speaking to someone, and his voice sounded to the wildly cheering Hilda like 'harps in the air'. On climbing down, the triumphant Solness kissed the girl and promised to come again in ten years' time, when he would make her a princess and present her with a whole kingdom.

All she experienced after the Master-Builder's feat (symbolic of one's ascent to the higher realms of consciousness) may have been only a fantasy, a day-dream of an imaginative and highly strung girl. But she believed in it and took its unspoken contents so seriously that ten years later the 'princess' herself suddenly turned up in order to claim her kingdom. Solness, however, was no longer the man she had known up there in the North. Nor did he now build churches with steeples surging into the skies—he was much too dizzy to climb into his former heights. His occupation during all those intervening years had been very much *terre-à-terre*; but it gave ample scope to his talent and rewarded him, moreover, with unrivalled fame. Yet for some mysterious reason he was never allowed to combine his calling with happiness and joy, that is with life in all its fullness. The more active he was in his vocation, the more had he to suffer and to make other people suffer as well. Every single step forward had to be paid for by some sacrifice or other. And this is how he described to Hilda his own rise to wealth and glory.

'He [the "Master"] wanted to give me the chance of becoming an accomplished master in my own sphere—so that I might build all the more glorious churches for Him. . . . Then I saw plainly why He had taken my little children from me. It was that I should have nothing else to attach myself to. No such thing as love and happiness, you understand. I was to be only master-builder—nothing else. And all my life long I was to go on building for Him.'

A synthesis of one's calling and the joy of life thus proved a much too complicated problem in practice. Unable to choose joy and happiness at the expense of his calling, Solness was compelled to choose his calling at the expense of happiness. But after the loss of his two children—when the sacrifice had become too high, Solness rebelled against the 'Master' in the name of his own personal will and independence. He rebelled on the very day when Hilda was so thrilled by his ascent to the top of the church-tower.

'First of all, I searched and tried my own heart—then I did the impossible—I no less than He. . . . I had never before been able to climb a great, free height. But that day I did it. . . . And when I stood there, high over everything, and was hanging the wreath over the vane, I said to Him: "Hear me, Thou Mighty One! From this day forward I will be a free builder—I, too, in my own sphere—just as Thou in Thine. I will never again build any more churches for Thee—only homes for human beings." '

Solness, like Rosmer, gave up his old valuations for the sake of the new ones. In the same way as Rosmer wanted to descend into the realm of ordinary human beings in order to ennoble them through joy, Solness decided to build homes for them to be happy in: 'Cosy, comfortable, bright homes, where father and mother, and the whole troop of children can live in safety and gladness, feeling what a happy thing it is to be alive in the world—and most of all to belong to each other—in great things and small.' But while building homes for others, he had to forgo the home that might have been his own—the home with happy parents and children. Later, after having seen too much of human nature and of the world, he could not but come to the conclusion that 'building homes for human beings is not worth sixpence. Men have no use for these homes of theirs—to be happy in. And I shouldn't have any use for such a home, if I had one.' For he was not and could not be happy. His egotistic rebellion against the 'Master' had only made things worse: in so far as—devoid of a supra-individual outlet—he had to fall back upon his own self with all its doubts and fears, which landed him in a crisis he was unable to cope with. He felt he had to revalue his vocation once again. But he was no longer equal to such a task. It was at this point that Hilda Wangel stepped into his life and fate.

IV

Even before Hilda 'knocked at the door', Solness had discovered, to his own grief, that to remain stuck in one's own self meant to be imprisoned. His descent proved less satisfying than his former 'romantic' heights which had no ties with ordinary earthly life. So he came to the conclusion that the only thing to do was to be firmly planted here on earth, while yet striving towards the heights, i.e. towards all the spiritual attainments accessible to man. Hence his strange idea of building houses with church-towers that 'point up into the free air. With the vane at a dizzy height.' He had built such a house for himself, but he would not think of climbing personally the height of its tower to hang the wreath. It was not only approaching old age that made him so reluctant, but the curious irrational side of life in general. There were so many fears and other disturbing things, including his own 'insecurity of conscience' which often made him confuse all the values of good and evil.

'Oh, there are devils innumerable abroad in the world, Hilda, that one never sees. Good devils and bad devils; light-haired devils and black-haired devils. If only you could always tell whether it is the light or the dark ones that have got hold of you! Ho-ho! Then it would be simple enough!'

What Hilda had brought to the Master-Builder was the notion of that robust conscience which, instead of withdrawing from, or succumbing to, realities, prefers to rise above them: to 'climb as high as one can build', but with one's feet firmly planted in life. Solness feels how her faith and daring have infected his will, but whenever he wants to rise, his own feeling of guilt and fear of retribution makes him dizzy.

SOLNESS: It is hopeless, Hilda. The luck is bound to turn. A little sooner or a little later. Retribution is inexorable.

HILDA (*in distress putting her hands over her ears*): Don't talk like that! Do you want to kill me? To take from me what is more than life?

SOLNESS: And what is that?

HILDA: The longing to see you great. To see you with a wreath in your hand, high, high up upon a church-tower.

This is how she demands from him the promised kingdom in which she wants him to build for her the 'loveliest thing in the world', that is a castle in the air—'with a clear outlook on all sides, so that I can see far—far around.' Instead of being a shelter for escapists and people with a dizzy conscience, that castle should soar in the height yet have a firm foundation on the earth below. The kingdom demanded by Hilda is really the 'third empire', formulated in her own naïvely spontaneous manner. For this she needs not only a brave but also a regenerated Solness. Regeneration, however, comes from living faith, and not from the scepticism of a wavering 'sickly conscience'. It is faith the Master-Builder lacks. Hence his fear and apprehension.

v

Spurred on by Hilda, Solness the creator finally decides to test his courage, despite the anxiety of his terror-stricken wife and the doubt of his younger rivals who are waiting for their chance. He hopes to 'climb as high as he could build'; to reach, in fact, the pinnacle of consciousness accessible to man—'with a clear outlook on all sides.' He also wants his triumph to mark a new phase in his self-realization: by merging his calling with all the joy and happiness for which he has been longing so far in vain—a new echo of the 'third empire'. But what he needs above everything for such a feat is that Hilda (a symbol of the future, of the 'dawning day') should not waver in her faith in him even when he himself is beset by doubts.

SOLNESS: You must go on believing in me.
HILDA: Then let me see you stand free and high up!
SOLNESS (*sadly*): Oh, Hilda—it is not every day that I can do that.
HILDA (*passionately*): I will have you do it. I will have it! (*Imploringly*.) Just once more, Mr. Solness! Do the impossible once again!
SOLNESS (*stands and looks deeply into her eyes*): If I try it, Hilda, I will stand there and talk to him as I did that time before. . . . I will say to him: 'Hear me, Mighty Lord—Thou may'st judge me as seems best to thee. But hereafter I will build nothing but the loveliest thing in the world—build it together with a princess whom I love.' And then I will say to him: 'Now I shall go and throw my arms round her and kiss her—many, many times,' I will say. Then I will wave my hat—and come down to the earth—and do so as I said to him. . . . The princess shall have her castle.

Solness did climb the tower. Yet having done so in his own name and with a challenge in his heart, he could not find, this time

either, the right words with which to address the Lord of Life.
When he was right on the top waving his hat, Hilda heard again
'harps in the air'. But during his triumph the Master-Builder
suddenly reeled. There was a cry of horror in the crowd below,
and his body crashed to the ground. Instead of the victor he
became the victim.

XIII

EMPTY HEIGHTS

I

SOLNESS in *The Master Builder* failed to reach that realm of the 'third empire' where his inner contradictions might have been solved, or at least superseded by a new type of consciousness. Had he not perished as he did, his old dilemma would have turned up again, sooner or later, exacting the same heavy price for his calling—and through no fault of his. He seemed to be in the grip of some mysterious power which used him as its medium, while holding him yet responsible for everything he did to himself and to others. His feeling of regret and of guilt before life became the heavier to him because he knew that there was no liberating atonement, but only the kind of retribution that maims and crushes. The situation resulting from it is described symbolically by the sculptor Rubek—Solness's counterpart in *When We Dead Awaken*:

'In front, beside a fountain, sits a man weighed down with guilt, who cannot free himself from the earth-crust. I call him remorse for a forfeited life. He sits there and dips his fingers in the purling stream —to wash them clean—and he is gnawed and tortured that never, never will he succeed. Never in all eternity will he attain to freedom and the new life. He will remain for ever imprisoned in his hell.'

It is a far cry from this lament in Ibsen's last play to Falk's naïvely romantic struggles for Ideals in *Love's Comedy*, or to Brand's deified one-track Will. One is reminded of the determinism cropping up in *Emperor and Galilean*—with the 'guilt-complex' added to it.

After a long and successful literary career, the aged Ibsen must have felt as puzzled by the enigma of life and personality as did Rosmer, Solness and Rubek. The devotion to his task and calling brought him fame, but little joy and happiness. His attempts to integrate the two in a higher synthesis only led him to further disappointments. And so did his endeavours to extract some meaning from it all. A religious approach, say, in the style of

Kierkegaard, was out of the question in his case, since he lacked the requisite turn of mind. Nor did his intellectual honesty allow him for a moment to impose upon himself and to parade the convictions or attitudes he could not believe in. His scepticism was not so much a method with him as a factor of inner integrity which impelled him to keep his eyes open and not accept anything on credit.

With all that he preserved his incurable idealistic temperament, his notion of the mystery of life, and his equally strong moral sense, which always made him take his stand on a level precluding any compromises with the 'earth-crust' in its less palatable aspects. His longings remained directed towards the heights, in spite of his suspicion that the heights themselves were empty, or most probably empty. Hence the rarified yet wistfully cold atmosphere in his last plays, among which *Little Eyolf* has a niche of its own.

II

However static *Little Eyolf* may appear on the surface, it still remains one of Ibsen's most carefully thought out and worked out plays. Apart from the calamity at the end of the first act, there are no happenings in it—only discussions and conversations. This does not prevent it, however, from being as rich in content and ideas as it is intense in psychology. In the centre is again the motif of human responsibility, round which there are grouped a few other Ibsenian dilemmas. These are arranged in such a way as to express all the more powerfully the nature of the inner change, undergone by Alfred and Rita Allmers after the loss of their only son Eyolf.

When Eyolf was a baby he fell from the table and became a cripple at the moment his parents were indulging in sexual passion. This penalty for their egoism was not heeded by either of them. Later, they both saw in the limping little boy a constant reminder of something unpleasant and shameful. They instinctively kept avoiding him, until one day, Alfred suddenly changed his attitude towards his nine-year-old son and decided to become a real father to him. But obstacles arose at once. The passionate and possessive Rita wanted her husband's affection all to herself. She resented the mere idea of having to share it with Eyolf.

There is nothing of Solness's tragic hardness in Alfred Allmers. He is nearer to Rosmer—at least in his brooding self-centredness and passivity. What he shares with both is, however, his puritan 'sickly conscience', which never leaves him in peace. Like Rosmer (before Beata's suicide) he has to put up with an impetuously sensuous wife, while he himself is rather frigid in this respect, and, at any rate, not quite adjusted to Rita. One of the reasons why he had married her was her wealth, which enabled him, amongst other things, to help his foster-sister Asta, and also gave him the leisure necessary for his life-task: the writing of a 'great thick book', *On Human Responsibility*. Alfred's attachment to Asta, whose company he prefers to that of his wife, takes us back to Rosmer and his fondness for Rebecca. And like Rosmer, he suddenly became a convert, intent on replacing his former life-task by a new and more important one.

The change came over him during his solitary wanderings in the mountains, where he had lost his way. Expecting the worst, he clearly felt the company of his fellow-traveller, Death, but later found the right track again and was saved. Under the weight of that experience he began to see a number of things—his 'great thick book' included—in a new light. So he decided on the spot that instead of theorizing about responsibility, he would practise it in his life. Was not the happiness of the crippled little Eyolf, who had always been a 'stranger boy' to his guilty parents, more relevant than any books or treatises? Without delay, he hurried home in order to turn his resolve into practice and to devote all his energies to Eyolf's future. 'I have been too much taken up by myself and by all these morbid, distorted, baseless fancies that I, myself, had some special mission in the world. Something of extreme importance and moment—something that concerns myself alone,' Ibsen makes him state in the notes for the play. Anyway, on his return Alfred sets out to become a true father and to develop the rich possibilities in Eyolf's soul.

> I will foster all the noble germs in his nature—make them blossom and bear fruit. And I will do more than that! I will help him to bring his desires into harmony with what is attainable before him. . . . Eyolf shall carry on my life-work—if he wants to. Or he shall choose one that is altogether his own. Perhaps that would be best. At all events, I shall let mine rest as it is.

It is here that Rita's jealousy comes in. Such a change in Alfred does not please her passionate full-blooded nature, and she reacts accordingly. During her altercation with Alfred, the limping little boy, as though spell-bound, follows the Rat-Wife (one of Ibsen's obscure symbols, vaguely reminiscent of the Pied Piper of Hamelin) right down to the pier. At the moment when Rita, claiming Alfred's love for herself alone, goes so far as to wish that Eyolf had never been born, the boy slips into the sea and is drowned. The only thing rescued is the floating crutch—a memento of his parents' guilt. This calamity marks the beginning of the inner drama of Rita and Alfred Allmers. The rest of the play deals with their reaction to Eyolf's death, or rather with its moral effect upon them. For Eyolf, though dead, is all the time invisibly present and, in fact, dominates the play.

III

Both parents are stunned by their child's death. The idea that they themselves may have been morally responsible for it does not at first enter their heads. The suddenness, the cruelty and the stupidity of it all is past their comprehension, and for a long time they are unable to discover any sense in it.

'Can you conceive the meaning of a thing like this?' [Alfred asks his foster-sister Asta at the beginning of the second act.] 'For after all there must be a meaning in it. Life, existence—destiny, cannot be so utterly meaningless.'

'Oh, who can say anything with certainty about these things, my dear Alfred?'

'No, no; I believe you are right there. Perhaps the whole thing is just haphazard—taking its own course, like a drifting wreck without a rudder. I dare say that is how it is. At least, it seems very like it.'

He is not sure about it. But supposing there is something more behind Eyolf's death, what is it then? Punishment for Rita's egoism and sensuality? But if so, why was it that the innocent little Eyolf had to pay for it, too? And why was he not saved by other boys on the pier—all of them good swimmers? 'The whole thing is utterly groundless and meaningless. And yet the order of the world requires it.'

There follow ugly and embittered mutual reproaches between the two parents. Alfred does not mind saying to his wife that her egoistic impulses were at the root of it. Whereupon Rita, who knows a thing or two about his hidden vanity, flings at him the remark that in his own way he was no less of an egoist than she. With subtle malice she interprets even his sudden decision to give up writing his book and to devote his life to Eyolf as an act of egoism in disguise:

'Because you were consumed with mistrust of yourself. Because you had begun to doubt whether you had any great vocation to live for in the world. . . . And then you needed something to fill up your life. . . . That was why you wanted to make a prodigy of poor little Eyolf. . . . Look into yourself! Search out all that lies under—and behind your action.'

'Have you found out this about me, too?'

But altercations of this kind do not help them to solve the riddle or the meaning of Eyolf's death. Only when they realize that they must look for a solution within themselves—in their past guilt with regard to Eyolf and in their present need of atonement— a change seems to be taking place in both of them. The calamity begins to assume a meaning in their eyes: even if the idea of retribution, which they eventually accept, is nearer to the mechanical working of the law of Karma than to Christian spirit. Though prompted by a strong moral impulse, their self-condemnation yet occurs in a void, as it were, and outside any deeper religious consciousness. It is a doomsday that leads to awakening without resurrection. 'Judgment upon you and me. . . . And what we call sorrow and heartache—is really the gnawing of conscience, Rita, nothing else.'

Similarly to Rosmer and Rebecca, they do not believe in a Judge above them; yet they, too, bend under a 'strange law', the acceptance of which affects their hearts and minds. The same suffering which at first made them so bitter towards each other, gradually purifies both of them. But the moral height which they have thus ascended is cold and empty. 'An empty void on all sides—wherever I look. . . .' No wonder that Rita is anxious to fill this void with a would-be task; with 'something that might counterbalance the loss of happiness,' as Ibsen wrote in his notes. 'Nothing that would equal happiness. But something that might make life livable.'

It is a modest demand indeed; a demand which has little in common with Brand's sweeping 'all or nothing'. But anything is better than an 'empty void on all sides'. Rita's expedient actually does not go beyond a decision on her part to educate those very urchins who had failed to save Eyolf, although they could have done so. And in this she is joined by her husband, since he, too, has his own void to fill.

'We have a heavy day of work before us, Rita.'
'You will see—that now and then a Sabbath peace will descend upon us.'

IV

The finale is thus not unlike that of Chekhov's *Uncle Vanya*: resignation under the cover of hard work. In this case the stress is on philanthropy—due, perhaps, also to the retarded awakening of Rita's mother-instinct which, after the loss of her child, she now transfers to other children. Be this as it may, her former full-blooded attachment to life is gone. No longer earth-bound as before, she is now free to look, together with her husband, 'upwards towards the stars and the great silence'. It is not the silence of life reposing in itself, but that of resigned despair.

As though anxious to make up for the melancholy of it, Ibsen gives a rather 'positive' contrast in the young roadmaker and Asta's admirer Borgheim. An active meliorist by nature, Borgheim has no time for brooding over insoluble problems. He looks for joy and happiness only in constructive tasks, the fulfilment of which is a reward in itself. 'Oh, what a glorious world this is—and what a joy it is to be a road-maker in it!' But his naïve optimism does not prevent us from hearing, at the end of this play, the muted melody of Alfred's 'fellow-traveller' in the mountains. And the melody becomes much louder in Ibsen's last two works, *John Gabriel Borkman* and *When We Dead Awaken*, where it actually expands into a regular 'dance of the dead'.

XIV

THE 'DANSE MACABRE'

I

THE law of retribution asserts itself in *John Gabriel Borkman* without any loopholes. The play shows certain minor gaps in technique, without losing however any of its poetic or dramatic power. One of its strong points is the conjured up 'atmosphere' of life's winter, and of desolation which dominates the play from start to finish—with Borkman as the central figure. The miner's son, John Gabriel Borkman, had sacrificed (no less than the master-builder Solness) everything to his calling and to his insatiable will to power. Ambitious as he was, he soon rose in the world and set out to liberate the untold riches buried in the bowels of the earth. 'I had power in my hands. And then I felt the irresistible vocation within me. Imprisoned millions lay all over the country.' He felt that to free those millions was his life-task, his mission. And when he set out to free them, he was by no means acting from sheer vain-glory. His aim was to achieve thereby a prosperous, joyful and happier life in wider and wider circles—like Johannes Rosmer. But in his eagerness to make a short cut to all the sources of power in the land, Borkman stumbled over the letter of the law and became a social outcast. This was, of course, only the external cause of his downfall. Its deeper inner reason was his betrayal of Ella—the sweetheart whom he had given up (like Bernick in *The Pillars of Society*) in order to marry her wealthy sister Gunhild, and thus realize the more quickly all the schemes by means of which he hoped to satisfy his calling. 'What you held dearest in the world you were ready to barter away for gain,' Ella reproaches him years later. 'That is the double crime you have committed. You have done to death all the gladness of life in me.'

Borkman was, however, of a tough mettle. He may have been condemned by law; but in his own judgment, far from being a criminal, he was only a financial Napoleon who became 'maimed in the first battle'. He found enough extenuating circumstances to acquit himself and even to expect a restitution to his former glory.

It is in this mood that he is first presented to us. Forgotten by the world and ostracized by his wife and his only son Erhart, he walks —'like a sick wolf'—up and down his lonely room day in, day out. The only person who comes to chat with him now and then is the pathetically comic Foldal: a victim of Borkman's financial adventures, but too weak, too good-natured, for any rancour. The two old men sponge on their pretended mutual faith in each other, but it is to no purpose. Borkman knows that his wife and his young son (a student) resent too much the shame he has brought upon his family ever to come and see him, but he is reconciled to that. He has never had anything in common with his wife, so what difference does it make? Suddenly Ella, on whose charity the entire Borkman family has subsisted for years, comes to Christiania from her retreat in the provinces, and her arrival is the immediate cause of the events that follow.

A grey-haired spinster, frustrated and mortally ill at that, Ella has undertaken the long journey in order to persuade Erhart, who owes his education and everything else to her, to join her in her loneliness and thus alleviate the last weeks of her life. A heated argument on account of Erhart follows between the two sisters. Ella, with her meek and generous disposition, and the hard despotic Gunhild—both lay claim upon the young man. But he intends to live his life in his own way. Neither his mother's plans nor those of his aunt make any difference to what he himself wants to do. This is why Ella's visit leaves him cool. But it makes quite an upheaval in his father's fate. For no sooner does old Borkman confront his one-time sweetheart after such a lapse of time than he decides to pull himself together by his own efforts, without waiting any longer for restitutions from without.

'I have been close to the verge of death. But now I have awakened. I have come to myself. A whole life lies before me yet. I can see it awaiting me, radiant and quickening.'
'Never dream of life again! Lie quietly where you are.'

Thus retorts Gunhild, who during all those years has been preparing a living monument over his grave. The monument is to be Erhart with his mission to restore the family name through a life so pure and high that her husband's 'burrowing in the dark' should be forgotten once and for all. But Erhart is not a missionary. He is young; he is in love; and all he really cares for is to snatch from

9

life as much happiness (or what he understands by it) as possible, without bothering about any tasks or missions.

'I am young! That is what I never realized before; but now the knowledge is tingling through every vein in my body. I will not work! I will only live, live, live. For happiness, mother.'

It is during Erhart's flight from all those living dead towards his rather questionable happiness that the covered sledge with the 'younger generation' in it runs over old Foldal—to the grim amusement of Borkman, who makes the apposite remark: 'Oh, we are all of us run over, sometime or other in life.' But he adds: 'The proper thing is to jump up again, and let no one see you are hurt.' For after his son's departure he himself has suddenly decided to jump up again and brave the 'storm of life' alone, at his own risk, in order to work his passage back to power and glory. Like an escaped slave, he rushes out into the winter night, and is anxiously followed by Ella—that pathetic shadow of her former self. From the top of the hill, so familiar to both of them, the two one-time lovers survey together the dreamland of their youth, now buried in the snow. Borkman, half-raving, listens to the magic call of voices coming from his vast kingdom in the earth, and whispers

'I love you, unborn treasures yearning for the light! I love you, love you, love you.'

'Yes, your love is still down there, John. But here, in the light of the day, here there was a living, warm, human heart that throbbed and glowed for you. And this heart you crushed. Oh, worse than that! Ten times worse! You sold it . . . And therefore, I prophesy to you, John Gabriel Borkman—you will never enter in triumph into your cold, dark kingdom.'

Her prophecy comes true on the spot. No longer accustomed to the cold fresh air, Borkman has a stroke. A 'hand of ice' clutches at his heart and kills him. The law of retribution, or—for that matter—of Karma, has had its way.

'It was rather the cold that killed him,' [Ella Rentheim whispers to her sister, Mrs. Borkman.]
'The cold, you say? The cold—that had killed him long ago.'
'Yes—and changed us two into shadows.'
'You are right there.'

III

The feeling of coldness, isolation and of an utter impasse in one permeates also Ibsen's last play, or the 'epilogue' as he calls it, *When We Dead Awaken*. Its hero, the sculptor Rubek is, however, nearer to Solness than to Borkman: in so far as he, too, realizes that mere artistic vocation which is not integrated with life, thrives at the expense of life; at the expense of happiness and joy. Like Solness, Rubek had once groped towards the realm of the 'third empire', the possibility of which he symbolized in his statue of the Resurrection Day. But he failed in his efforts in no less tragic a manner than the Master-Builder.

Rubek, too, has a cardinal guilt to atone for. In his urge to realize himself through his calling, he sacrificed to art everything—including the love of Irene, who, day after day, had sat with devotion for his statue. Yet the 'resurrection', as visualized in his work of art, was not and could not be achieved by him in life. The statue, which had been created at the expense of love, spread Rubek's fame all over the world. But restlessness, dissatisfaction and lack of happiness set in as the punishment or retribution that was in store for him. Rubek and Irene (like Borkman and Ella) meet years after they had parted: he as a celebrated artist, and she as a patient convalescing, after a period of insanity, in a mountain sanatorium where, still half-demented, she walks about like a ghost and suffers from the fixed idea that she is dead. They recognize each other, and Irene's accusations do not differ in essence from those of Ella in the previous play.

IRENE: I fell down at your feet and served you, Arnold! But you—you—
RUBEK: I never wronged you. Never, Irene!
IRENE: Yes, you did! You did wrong to my innermost unborn nature——
RUBEK (*starting back*): I——!
IRENE: Yes, you! I exposed myself wholly and unreservedly to your gaze——
RUBEK: I was an artist, Irene.
IRENE: That is just it. That is just it. . . . The work of art first, then the human being.
RUBEK: You must judge me as you will; but at that time I was utterly dominated by my great task and exultantly happy in it.
IRENE: And you achieved your great task, Arnold.

9*

RUBEK: Thanks and praise be to you, I achieved my great task. I wanted to embody the pure woman as I saw her awakening on the Resurrection Day . . . filled with a sacred joy at finding herself unchanged—she, the woman of earth—in a higher, happier, freer region —after the long, dreamless sleep of death. I fashioned her in your image, Irene.

IRENE: And then you were done with me. . . . But you have forgotten the most precious gift.

RUBEK: The most precious——? What gift was that?

IRENE: I gave you my young, living soul. And that gift left me empty within—soulless. (*Looking at him with a fixed stare.*) It was that I died of, Arnold. . . . When I had served you with my soul and with my body— when the statue stood there finished—our child as you called it—then I laid at your feet the most precious sacrifice of all—by effacing myself for all time. . . .

RUBEK: Was it jealousy that moved you then?

IRENE (*coldly*): I think it was rather hatred.

RUBEK: Hatred! Hatred for me?

IRENE: Yes, for you—for the artist who had so lightly taken a warm-blooded body, a young human life, and worn the soul out of it—because you needed it for your work of art.

As Irene points out, she, too, had a life to live and a human destiny of her own to fulfil: the destiny of motherhood, of her devotion to children from the man she loved. 'And all that I let slip—gave it all up in order to make myself your bondswoman. Oh, it was self-murder—a deadly sin against myself. And that sin I can never expiate. . . . I ought never to have served you— poet,' she reproaches him scornfully: in the way the aged and frustrated Svanhild might have reproached, after many years, the successful poet Falk.

Irene committed 'self-murder' by allowing her personality to be used only as a means for somebody else's task, for a work of art, which left her 'empty within'. But Rubek, too, who had turned her sacrifice into a work of art and a mere 'priceless episode', failed to create anything truly significant, once she had vanished from his orbit. The repressed eros took revenge upon the artist by depriving him of inspiration. Rubek won honours and riches; later he married his young wife Maia; but the creative *élan* he had known in Irene's company never came back again. His talent was wasted henceforth on modelling the busts of plutocrats with pompous animal-like faces peering through their masks.

'Men's laurels and incense nauseated me, till I could have rushed away and hidden myself in the depths of the woods. . . . All the talk about the artistic missions and so forth, began to strike me as being very empty, and meaningless at bottom.'

'Then what would you put in its place?'

'Life, Maia.'

But life is irretrievable. Even if it were not so, mere pleasures in those lower realms, where the satyr-like hunter Ulfheim and Maia felt so much at home, would hardly have attracted either Rubek or Irene. Rubek's secret urge, like that of Solness or of Ibsen himself, is one towards the fullness of existence in that 'higher, happier, freer region' of consciousness where there is no longer any gap between one's calling and the happiness of life. It is for the sake of such fullness that he decides to challenge his destiny. But, like Solness once again, he does it in his own name. The only difference is that the high tower is replaced by a steep mountain (also provided with a tower), with dangerous corners, 'where you can neither get forward nor back. And then you stick fast! Mountain-fast, we hunters call it. . . .' Without heeding Ulfheim's warning, Rubek and Irene continue their ascent. But the futility of their belated effort begins to dawn on both of them. The lives they have wasted, the ardour of youth, of love and passion—all this is beyond recall, and it is no use pretending that it can be recaptured. The two of them are like two dead 'clay-cold' bodies playing with each other.

'The love that belongs to the earth—the beautiful, miraculous earth-life—that is dead in both of us. . . . The desire for life is dead in me, Arnold. Now I have risen. And I look for you. And then I see that you and life lie dead—as I have lain. . . . The young woman of your Resurrection Day can see all life lying on its bier.'

One is reminded of the cold and cruel void around Alfred Allmers and Borkman. Rubek feels the truth of Irene's remark, and despair sounds in the very defiance of his answer:

'Then let the two of the dead—us two—for once live life to its uttermost—before we go down to our graves again.'

But even this is not granted to them. As they struggle on, through the mist to the 'summit of the tower that shines in the sun-rise', retribution comes, as in *Brand*, in the shape of a rolling avalanche which buries them both.

V

The inner kinship of this play with *The Master Builder* and *John Gabriel Borkman* need not be stressed. In all three we see a kind of 'doomsday' held over one's calling. Nemesis works because life, the 'beautiful, miraculous earth-life', has been left out of account. The problem of integrating art and life thus arose most acutely in Ibsen's mind when life, with all its potential joy, happiness and warmth, had already been left behind, and when even world-fame could not compensate him for what he had missed while serving art at the expense of everything else. As he had not succeeded in realizing himself fully through the longed-for integration, he too—like Solness and Rubek—remained inwardly split. His work was in essence one continuous attempt to cope with this cleavage, as well as a self-reproach because of his failure. All he could do in his 'epilogue' was to pass a final judgment upon himself and to acknowledge his defeat.

Technically, *When We Dead Awaken* marks a considerable ebbing away of Ibsen's creative power—a process which had set in with *The Master Builder*. There are also logical inconsistencies in this play. Most of its *dramatis personae* are shadows rather than three-dimensional characters—as in an 'expressionist' allegory which it often resembles. Ibsen obviously wrote this final judgment over his work and his life in a hurry, and finished it none too soon: on March 15th, 1900 he had a stroke, and another in January of the following year. Something must have gone wrong with his mind, too; for eventually he forgot even how to write. Like a little schoolboy, he began to learn again how to scrawl the letters of the alphabet. He died on May 23rd 1906, at the age of seventy-eight.

CONCLUSION

THE days when Ibsen's plays were a sensation both on and off the stage are now past. This does not diminish their intrinsic value—it only puts them in a right perspective, which is all to the good. Ibsen the playwright has certainly withstood the test of time, and his contribution to the modern drama in general is beyond dispute. G. B. Shaw, Luigi Pirandello, Gerhart Hauptmann, Anton Chekhov (to name only a few)—they all owed some aspects of their art to Ibsen. As to the minor playwrights indebted to him, their name is legion. Yet however much all this is now taken for granted, the personality of Ibsen in its relation to his work is still puzzling enough to leave room for further inquiry. The more so because he himself stressed the fact that he wrote only from intimate personal experience.

Like Dostoevsky, Tolstoy, Nietzsche, Kierkegaard, and Strindberg, Ibsen too was essentially a 'schizophrenic' modern. Less complicated than the above-mentioned 'big four', and also less confused than Strindberg, he represents for this very reason a more accessible example of that division and self-division which, since the romantic movement in particular, has been so marked a feature of our European mentality and culture as a whole. He had to contend not only with the age and the society in which he lived, but above all with the numerous 'trolls' (his expression) within his own self. And however big the price his struggle had cost him, he yet failed to achieve the inner unity he so ardently longed and worked for.

The power with which Ibsen the artist stated his personal dilemma in terms of universal values is the measure of his genius. It was through his art that some of the basic problems of human conscience have become flesh. This is why his work can hardly be ignored by a generation which has to face not only the social but also the spiritual havoc wrought by the two ghastliest wars in history. Ibsen, whose creations were due to a series of inner crises, still remains one's valuable ally in a period which is but one vast query and crisis.

BIBLIOGRAPHY

I. SOME ENGLISH TRANSLATIONS OF IBSEN

Collected Works, edited by William Archer. London. Heinemann, 1906–10. 12 vols.

The Works of Henrik Ibsen, The Viking Edition. New York. Scribner's Sons, 1911. 13 vols.

Ibsen, Lyrics and Poems, translated by F. E. Garrett. New York. Dutton, 1913.

Ibsen's Lyrical Poems, selected and translated by R. A. Streatfield. London, 1902.

The Doll's House, The Wild Duck and The Lady from the Sea. London. Everyman's, 1910.

Ghosts and Two Other Plays (The Warriors at Helgeland, An Enemy of the People). London. Everyman's, 1911.

The Pretenders, Pillars of Society and Rosmersholm. London. Everyman's, 1913.

Four Plays (A Doll's House, Ghosts, The Wild Duck, The Master Builder), with an Introduction by Desmond MacCarthy. Nelson classics, 1941.

II. SOME WORKS ON IBSEN IN ENGLISH

Ibsen the Norwegian, by Muriel Bradbrook. London. Chatto and Windus, 1946.

Ibsen, The Intellectual Background, by W. Downs. Cambridge University Press, 1946.

Henrik Ibsen. A Bibliography of Criticism and Biography, by Ina T. E. Firkins. New York. The H. Wilson Co., 1921.

Ibsen, by E. W. Gosse. London. Hodder and Stoughton, 1907.

Henrik Ibsen. Plays and Problems, by Otto Heller. Boston. Houghton Mifflin, 1912.

Henrik Ibsen, by Archibald Henderson. 2 vols. New York. Kemerly, 1911.

Henrik Ibsen, a Critical Biography, by H. B. Jaeger. Chicago. McClurg, 1901.

The Life of Ibsen, by Halvdan Koht. 2 vols. London. Allen & Unwin, 1931.

Henrik Ibsen. A Critical Study, by R. Ellis Roberts. London. Secker, 1912.

The Quintessence of Ibsenism, by G. B. Shaw. London. Constable, 1891.

Ibsen's Dramatic Technique, by P. F. D. Tennant. Cambridge. Bowes, 1948.

Shakespeare and Ibsen, by H. G. Dalway Turnbull. Oxford. Blackwell, 1926.

The Modern Ibsen, by Hermann Weigand. London. Dent, 1925.

Ibsen the Master Builder, by A. E. Zucker. London. Thornton Butterworth, 1930.

INDEX

PRINTED BY
JARROLD AND SONS LTD.
NORWICH